More Love, Less Fear

A Memoir. A Love Story about a Husband,
a Wife, and the Deadly Disease of ALS.

ROBERT and **THERESA LEE**

BALBOA
PRESS
A DIVISION OF HAY HOUSE

Balboa Press books may be ordered through booksellers or by contacting:

Balboa Press
A Division of Hay House
1663 Liberty Drive
Bloomington, IN 47403
www.balboapress.com
1 (877) 407-4847

Because of the dynamic nature of the Internet, any web addresses or links contained in this book may have changed since publication and may no longer be valid. The views expressed in this work are solely those of the author and do not necessarily reflect the views of the publisher, and the publisher hereby disclaims any responsibility for them.

The author of this book does not dispense medical advice or prescribe the use of any technique as a form of treatment for physical, emotional, or medical problems without the advice of a physician, either directly or indirectly. The intent of the author is only to offer information of a general nature to help you in your quest for emotional and spiritual well-being. In the event you use any of the information in this book for yourself, which is your constitutional right, the author and the publisher assume no responsibility for your actions.

Any people depicted in stock imagery provided by Thinkstock are models, and such images are being used for illustrative purposes only. Certain stock imagery © Thinkstock.

Printed in the United States of America.

ISBN: 978-1-5043-2526-4 (sc)
ISBN: 978-1-5043-2528-8 (hc)
ISBN: 978-1-5043-2527-1 (e)

Library of Congress Control Number: 2014922394

Balboa Press rev. date: 02/03/2015

For Theresa—my angel who now watches over me. One day we will dance together again.

For my mom—thank you for giving me your constant smile and easygoing nature.

For my sons, Tim, Alex, and Justin— you give me hope for the future.

For the family and friends who saw us through our darkest hour—thank you.

A short note on names:

Our journey included many who were integral to our journey. Out of common courtesy, I have used pseudonyms in only a handful of instances.

Contents

Letter to the Reader..xi

Chapter 1   There Will Always Be Taxes to Pay......................1
Chapter 2   We "Injoyed" Ourselves 13
Chapter 3   Preparing for the Test 27
Chapter 4   The Journey Is Heralded................................37
Chapter 5   We May Not Have Corner Vision, But
             We Still Drive......................................47
Chapter 6   The Third Party in Our Marriage 55
Chapter 7   When Life Dumps Fertilizer on You,
             You Grow...65
Chapter 8   Our New Normal.......................................71
Chapter 9   Sometimes You Need Darkness to See
             the Light 89
Chapter 10   Trump Tragedy with Triumph.......................... 105
Chapter 11   Have Faith No Matter What Form It Takes...... 119
Chapter 12   Even in a Storm Lies a Center of Calm 131
Chapter 13   Pulling Back from the Brink......................... 145
Chapter 14   You're Stronger than You Know 155
Chapter 15   An Iota of Hope Is Still Hope 165
Chapter 16   Trapped in a Miracle................................ 173
Chapter 17   Of Sacrifice and Gratitude......................... 181
Chapter 18   And Then We Let Go.................................. 191

Epilogue..201
How ALS Lived with Me for Twelve Years 207
    Health Tips and Observations..................................208

Letter to the Reader

My name is Robert. The story I'm about to tell you does not have a happy ending. As you turn the pages, you'll learn how I lost my wife and the woman I love to a monster of a disease.

If there are words to describe how cruel ALS is, then I don't know them. ALS (amyotrophic lateral sclerosis), or Lou Gehrig's disease, is a progressive neurodegenerative disease that cuts you down slowly, bit by bit. One day you can walk. The next day, not so well. Eventually your legs become lifeless limbs. Your speech, once clear and brilliant, becomes an inaudible gurgle and is eventually silenced forever. And on it marches. ALS hijacks every muscle in your body until you can no longer swallow or breathe. And as if that isn't cruel enough, all the while you are lucid—fully aware that you are disappearing one muscle at a time, completely awake as your body inches closer to a permanent state of nothingness. The disease can strike anyone—it has no racial, ethnic, or socioeconomic profile. There is no known cause, no known cure, and very little in the way of medical help or management of the symptoms. For the most part, all the patient can do is let it happen. All the caregiver can do is watch.

But while there is no happy ending to our story, there is a happy message.

There are three main reasons for writing this book. The first comes from Terri. She had always been about helping her fellow man. So it was no surprise to me or to anyone who knew her well that she wanted to chronicle her journey. "If it can help even one person," she'd say, "I need to share my story." But ALS had other plans, so Terri's book would have to wait until after she had taken her last breath. Fortunately, she left much of her research and letters for us to share with you now.

The second reason comes from me. This work is my public tribute to her. She filled me with so much love that I feel compelled to share it. I want to let others know that not only is it possible to have this kind of love, but also when you have it, you can be happy even in the worst of conditions. Yes, *happy*. To those who may be starting along the path that I have just ended as a caregiver, I hope this book becomes for you a bridge to strength and compassion. The road you have chosen to travel is not an easy one. Fatigue, frustration, resentment, and even anger ... you will feel all this, and more, at one end of the spectrum. At the other end are an abundance of joy, happiness, purpose—and, of course, love.

In the months that followed my wife's passing, I looked back and saw the trail of what I now understand to be the stepping-stones that led me to this journey. It was not altogether apparent while we were going through it, but they now sit there clearly mapped in my mind. This has forever changed the way I look at events or encounters that at first blush make no sense. Before Terri and ALS, I had always been intrigued with the notion that there is no such thing as a coincidence. If I had any doubts before, I no longer do. I am convinced that everything happens for a reason. *Everything*.

Third, I'd like to think of *More Love, Less Fear* as our final collaboration as husband and wife. This is the story of our last great adventure—our twelve-year relationship with a terminal illness that ended Terri's life, but not our love for one another. My beloved wife may no longer be by my side, but she will forever shape the way I see and live my life. It is her last and lasting gift to me, and one that I am honored to share.

At the end of the day, Terri and I not only accepted our circumstances, we embraced it and infused it with the love we had for one another. It was not always easy, but our conscious decision to choose love and positive emotions, regardless of what lay before us, kept us afloat to the very end. I can say without hesitation that Terri lived with ALS in relative peace, making the most of each day she awakened to see the faces of her loved ones around her.

More Love, Less Fear offers no magic solution with which to conquer ALS, although we certainly gave it our best shot. Once she had exhausted the help of Western medicine, Terri turned to a holistic approach, hoping that it would help prolong her life—which it did somewhat successfully. I call it a *success* because she lived until her last breath without the need for a breathing machine or feeding tube, and she enjoyed better than average health, ALS notwithstanding. Included at the end of this book are excerpts from her blog and notes for the book she had wanted to leave behind. They offer detailed information on some of the products she used, changes in her diet, and other health tips and guidelines. Whether you or someone you know is suffering from ALS or any other illness, Terri's self-help guide may be of some inspiration. Take from it whatever help you can. She certainly covered a lot of groundwork, which she was only too happy to pass on. That was her way.

I hope you'll stay with us as we share with you the roller-coaster journey that took us to our lowest and highest points as a married couple. To say it tested the mettle of our vows is to be flippant. The truth is that living with ALS made us confront and challenge the very concept of what it means to love someone unconditionally. It was a test unlike any other. And while in the end the disease conquered her body, it did not weaken or blemish our marriage. In fact, in many ways it strengthened it.

Most important, it reaffirmed something we had known all along: that living with gratitude is the most powerful lifestyle one can ever choose. ALS made us aware of all the blessings we had, from the simple to the grand. What we learned while living with this horrible disease is that it is better to work with it than attack it. Instead of fighting the rip current that was Terri's ALS, we tried to find some sense of calm by going with the flow. To a certain extent, it worked. It is my hope—as it was Terri's—that our story will help you with whatever rip currents may come your way.

One last note … Terri and I felt safe enough in our love to openly point out to each other personal faults that were less than desirable. Impatience was one of her biggest, in my opinion; it was a flaw she graciously admitted to having when I pointed it out to her. Toward the end of her life, she smiled one day and suggested that ALS was no doubt the best cure for her particular malady.

One of her criticisms of me was that I tend to fall so head over heels in love with a new idea or project, that I become almost too focused and overzealous. That project then becomes all I can talk about with every person to come my way. Oftentimes Terri would have to give me a little kick under the table as a reminder to take a breath and let the other person get a word in. During the course of writing this book, I'd often smile and wonder what she'd have thought if she knew I started it within days of laying her to rest, and that it was all I could think of until it was completed. And that's when I'd miss that soft smile of hers and that gentle tap under the table. I'd give anything to feel that loving reminder once again.

Blessed love,
Robert

Boast not thyself of tomorrow; for thou knowest
not what a day may bring forth.

—Proverbs 27:1

CHAPTER 1

There Will Always Be Taxes to Pay

Terri and I met in 1988 in the context of a bad business transaction that involved a mutual friend and a secondhand tractor.

At the time, I was living in my native Jamaica in an apartment in the heart of Ocho Rios, a popular tourist destination on the island's north coast. Blessed with the perfect balance of sunshine and seasonal rains, it was—and still is, in my opinion—an absolute paradise on earth. I also never took for granted the fact that I had the good fortune of being able to practically claim the Caribbean Sea as my front yard.

Early morning was the time of day I carved out for me. I had always enjoyed rising at 5:00 a.m., before the sun made its daily debut. Weather permitting, I'd start my days by going for a run along the jagged coastal roadway. Fitness and marathon training were my main passions then, and I'd work my entire schedule around them. Nothing thrilled me more than to dive into the cool air when most had not yet begun to stir, and when the morning dew still lightly frosted every leaf and bloom. At that early hour, it would be quiet enough that I could hear myself breathe, focus on my heartbeat, and feel the impact of my feet hitting the asphalt.

Five miles.
Don't stop now.
Nine miles.
No time to quit.
Ten miles.
The pain is just in your mind.
Make it disappear.
You can do it.

If there was one thing running had taught me over the years, it was this: just when I thought I had no more to give, if I pushed just a bit more, stuck it out a little bit longer, I would find the reserve I needed to see me through whatever task it was that had me in challenge mode.

Once my morning run was over, at about 7:00 a.m., I'd plunge into the watery field of blue and swim out as far as my body could take me. Those morning swims were my daily meditation.

Already thirty-eight years old, I was an active businessman with a penchant for multitasking. As I was graphic artist by training, one of my first ventures was a printing shop. Music was another first love, and I immediately combined the two by focusing on the entertainment industry. I serviced all the clients I could find, big and small—including my own band, which I'd started before the print shop ever came to be. I was the band's drummer—a decidedly untalented one, as it would soon turn out. Under normal conditions, I'd have been immediately terminated. And quite frankly, I could not have blamed my fellow music makers. I was that unimpressive. But since I owned all the equipment, I knew the others wouldn't fire me. Nevertheless, I stepped down in the name of progress and donned the manager's hat instead. That was my first lesson in business—own everything to ensure job security.

Yes, I loved sticking my fingers in all manner of pie, without discrimination. At one point I even became a distributor of Life Fitness exercise equipment. It all started with a friend of mine who owned a gym and needed to import equipment to fill it. Quick research put us in touch with a company owned by a fellow named Augie Nieto. The health guru to many a Hollywood star, Nieto was based in California and was the cofounder of Life Fitness, a company that manufactured the industry's first computerized fitness equipment. It was cutting-edge. As a fellow fitness aficionado, I was only too happy to make contact with Nieto's company and possibly meet this superstar of health and vitality.

My friend José and I made plans to attend a distributors' meeting, where we had the opportunity to meet Nieto briefly in person. He didn't disappoint. Tall and built like a small fortress, he was impressive from appearance alone. He oozed with a life force that made you want to kick your own into hyperdrive. Before long, my friend and I became Caribbean distributors for the company. Nieto himself would eventually move on, selling his successful company to Bally Manufacturing Corporation, the Chicago casino and fitness club giant.

Once our distributorship was settled, I turned my attention to real estate, focusing on my beloved Ocho Rios. "Go where your soul likes to rest," I always said. One of my property development projects eventually led me to purchase a woodworking shop. My thinking was, *Why buy doors and windows if I can make them myself?* The more pots I had on the fire, the happier I was. And it didn't matter whether or not I had experience in the field. I didn't mind jumping into just about anything, if I took a fancy to it. In fact, to be totally honest, I'd have to say that the thrill of the unknown was probably what drove me into most if not all of my ventures—including those that turned into adventures or, worse, "badventures." And I had had my fair share of those.

I freely admit that, to many, I seemed completely reckless and stuck in overdrive. The life I had led as a younger man often had many a head shaking. "Slow down, man," family and friends would counsel repeatedly. "You've got your whole life ahead of you. What's the big rush?" I can't say what pushed me so hard. I didn't particularly feel as if I was in a race against time, but I did feel in my bones that I needed to make good on the opportunities that were coming at me. But at the end of the day, I chalked it up to an aversion to inertia. I figured that life was like your heartbeat. If it wasn't moving up and down, then it was flatlining, and that definitely was bad news.

When Terri and I met, the latest addition to my juggling act was a residential development project that involved two-bedroom flats to be built on a picturesque rolling hill, just six minutes from the island's beach-famous coastline. The ink on the paperwork was barely dry, and already the project had claimed my time, undivided attention, and excited energy. I was ready to stick that shovel into the ground. And that Saturday seemed like as good a day as any to get started.

I didn't have to go searching through the Yellow Pages to find the tractor. I knew exactly where to go. I telephoned an acquaintance by the name of Fred. Fred confirmed that not only did he have the tractor I was looking for, it just so happened that it was available for purchase. Wouldn't it make more sense, he suggested, that I buy it from him instead of just borrowing it?

I remember attempting to stand my ground. I knew something about carpentry equipment due to the workshop I owned, but that was about it. Big machinery was definitely not my thing, and I felt no particular "tug" in my gut that this could be another winner.

And, yet, a minute later I heard myself agreeing to meet with him at my home the following day. Maybe it was the lazy feeling in the air. The sea breeze can have that effect on you. Maybe I just wasn't up for a protest that day. Or perhaps I simply hadn't had enough coffee by then. And then I heard a voice in my head say, *It's just a tractor, Robert. Don't overthink it.*

The following day, Fred arrived at my apartment at precisely 10:00 a.m. I was impressed at his punctuality, especially as it was a Sunday. But he wasn't alone. He had with him his girlfriend, Patty, and her sister, who was spending some time with them away from her home in Mandeville, a town a couple hours' drive south of Ocho Rios. Her name was Theresa, or "Terri," as she called herself. I am an admitted and helpless connoisseur of beautiful women. As a much younger man, I had been married—albeit very briefly—to a very attractive girl, with whom I had a son, Tim.

My eyes went into autopilot, immediately scanning this petite beauty as she brushed her long dark hair away from her face. To this day I can't remember what she wore, or whether she sat or remained standing. I remember only her smile. It flashed before me with eyes that almost seemed to dance. That smile was like an ignition key that kick-started my heart with a jolt I'd never quite known before. *Where in the world,* I thought to myself, *has this incredible woman been hiding all along?*

Our eyes locked in that instinctive way when physical attraction is undeniable, but we kept it light. At the time I was involved with a girl or two in Miami, so I made no overtures, tempted as I was. Terri, unbeknown to me, was still recovering from a bad breakup. In fact, it was the reason she had left her home in Mandeville for a spell.

Nevertheless, I engaged in the usual exchange of pleasantries to find out something—anything—about this woman. I learned that she had pursued a degree in computer studies in the 1980s at Ryerson University in Toronto, long before the word *computer* had become mainstream. But after a few years of working in her field, she felt an immediate and compelling urge to work with her hands. So she started a business with her brother and sister in, of all things, pottery. She could not have known then that she would have only another two decades left to use her hands. She had known nothing about the world of clay and ceramics, but she felt sure enough about it to jump in and learn. Now thirty-two, she managed to make a modest living from it, and she harbored no regrets about leaving her profession to chase her dreams and find real fulfillment.

I couldn't help but smile at the similarity between us. Her uncommon determination and respect for the instinctive were traits I rarely encountered in others. The reason for that gut message from the universe to literally put her hands to work would not make itself known for several years yet. Ironically, her brain—the part of her she had spent her early years shaping and developing while pursuing her degree—would be the only tool left to her once ALS had stripped her of everything else.

Meanwhile, Fred must have been sensing the advantageous distraction in the air, because he immediately proceeded with his buy-the-tractor campaign. I told him again that I didn't know the first thing about tractors or construction equipment, but he was ready for that argument. He sweetened the offer with the option of hiring one of his "experienced" mechanic operators to ensure a smooth transition. Under normal circumstances I would have smelled and heard the rat scurrying under the table. But my senses had already been compromised by the electricity in the air. In the end I didn't put up much of an argument. An hour later we were shaking hands on my acquisition of a spanking-brand-new-to-me used tractor.

The project didn't exactly start off well. Nor did the tractor. It broke down with a pitiful sputter within the first few days. My new employee made the unhappy diagnosis with little hesitation— it required a major and therefore expensive part. I should have picked up on his suspiciously immediate pronouncement, but I didn't. The same thing happened in week two, this time with another equally major and costly part. Meanwhile, Terri's image kept flashing through my mind.

We ran into each other a mere handful of times after that. But it wasn't until the Easter holiday that we finally acted on our mutual attraction. The Easter weekend is one of the island's major holidays, with a long list of local events from which to choose. One of the long-standing ones was a two-day stock-car road race that attracted the usual suspects: car enthusiasts, testosterone-charged guys, and lots of pretty girls in much-appreciated short shorts.

At the time I was in the middle of a contract with the Dover Raceway Club to build a spectator grandstand on the side of a hill, so I decided to go that weekend. I also happened to have the added incentive of a beautiful lady friend to show off; one of my girlfriends was visiting from Miami. She was a lovely girl—a tall, beautiful blonde with an amazing physique that usually won me the thumbs-up from friends. Since we had always enjoyed each other's company as well, I didn't hesitate to invite her, thinking it would be a fun day. But as soon as we arrived, I saw Terri.

My heart both sank and leapt. I knew I was in trouble. Terri was already at work as the volunteer roving accountant, collecting ticket and concession sales monies from the various vendors. She wore leg-revealing shorts that won my immediate attention and approval. I decided to try and strike up a conversation to test the waters. After a few minutes, encouraged by her relaxed bantering, I decided to take it a step further.

"With all that money you're carrying around, Terri, you're going to need some protection," I said. She laughed, clearly understanding that a pitch was on its way.

"And I suppose you have a suggestion?" she teased.

"As a matter of fact, yes!"

"Well, let's hear it then," she quipped lightly. "I don't have all day here! I'm a very busy woman."

"How about I be your bodyguard for the day?" I asked with a nervous laugh.

"Well, well! My own bodyguard," she said with a smirk. "Now, that's an offer I've never had!"

"No charge!" This time she met my flirtation with the most beautiful open smile I had ever seen.

"Are you sure you want to do that, Robert? Be my bodyguard, that is?"

"Yes, of course! Why not?"

"Well, you know what they say—be careful what you ask for. What if I end up being more than you bargained for?"

"Not a problem," I said. "I'm ready for the job."

She looked at me as if to size me up. It was only a few seconds' pause, but I thought it would never end. I could tell she was having a conversation with herself about me. She wasn't just playing. And then she smiled. "Okay, Robert," she said. "You're hired."

To this day I can still see her standing before me under the warm sun, laughing as if I'd just said the funniest thing she'd ever heard, brushing her hair back, tossing me that smile of hers ... acting on a lover's instinct. We could not have known then that one day I would literally become her body's caregiver and protector for the remainder of her life. When I think back to what was essentially our first private conversation, my hair stands on end.

Before setting off on my mission, I cashed in on a favor owed by asking a friend to look after my date. Already feeling guilty, but unwilling and unable to step away from Terri, I started walking alongside her, never allowing more than twelve inches of air between us.

Dover was mostly slopes and steep hills, with the flat portion reserved for the track. When a particularly difficult hill presented itself, I used it as an excuse to touch her for the first time. I placed both my hands on her hips to steady her as we climbed the tricky bank. She didn't protest. I reveled in the physical attraction between us, which was now clearly mutual and obvious to just about everyone—including the lady friend I had brought along. I knew I had some serious music to face.

The end of the day came much too quickly. Flashing a smile and planting a slow kiss on her cheek, I said good-bye to my charge. The time on my watch said it had been a long day. It had also been a hot one. By now most spectators were sporting red, irritated faces from too much sun, mixed in with sweat and layers of dust. I went through the thick crowd in search of my original date. Not surprisingly, she was drunk and not in the mood to even look at me. She didn't say much either when I dropped her off at the airport in Montego Bay the following day, although her eyes gave me an earful.

As soon as I dropped her off, I made a beeline back to Terri's just so I could see her, and maybe even persuade her to go out with me that night. I literally sat in front of her as she waded through her paperwork tallying the sales from the weekend's event. I told her that I wasn't leaving until she agreed to let me take her out. She feigned annoyance, but I saw through the glint in her eye that she understood the chase was on.

That night I took Patty and Terri to one of the hotel's nightclubs. I was a pretty competent dancer and wanted to show this woman something about me, if only on a superficial level. Music had always been magic for me—an instant mood lifter and a medicinal tonic at times. In fact, I can't remember letting a day go by without it. So I wanted her to see that rhythm resided in me. I wanted her to see my peacock dance, if you will … except that I had no idea my hen was about to outshine my performance. We spent a couple of hours on the dance floor, taking time out only to wash the thirst out of our throats with a few drinks. Terri would tell me later that she was thrilled to discover we shared an insatiable love of dancing. And so that's what Terri and I did on our first date—put our feet, legs, and arms to work as if it were our last dance ever. And it was on that dance floor that I knew with every fiber of my being that she was someone I could spend time with—really love—for the rest of my life.

I won't deny the fact that I felt like a cad about what I'd done to my visiting girlfriend. I *was* a cad. But there was nothing more to the discussion. I was drawn to Terri in the way that water finds the nearest escape—caught in complete surrender as the current of attraction swept me toward her. I didn't care. I was not about to deny my feelings for this woman, or miss the chance to journey with her wherever our relationship would take us.

It is a very simple principle. When you find the person who is meant for you, nothing else matters, and you don't allow anything to stand in your way. I had never known this kind of pull from love before. Nothing about this was cerebral. Everything about it was emotional. But it was much more than "love." It was a gut instinct, an unshakable belief that I was meant to be with this woman. And the problem with gut instincts is this: you can ignore them all you want, call them by a different name, cloak them with lies and distorted images, and even render them temporarily mute if you're able to.

You can do all of that, but you can never, ever quite shake it off.

Be careful how you think; your life is shaped by your thoughts.

—Proverbs 4:23

CHAPTER 2

We "Injoyed" Ourselves

It was a short but relentless pursuit. Our courtship read like a clichéd romance novel, complete with white-sand beaches, moonlight dinners, and spontaneous getaway trips off the island. Terri was the one for me. I didn't hesitate this time to do the right thing. I let the other two ladies I had been casually dating know that I was moving on for good. This was it. One took it graciously and remained friends with us. The other—my Dover date—couldn't wait to see the back of me. I couldn't fault her for it, of course, and I wished her well nevertheless. Everyone deserves happiness.

From the moment I met Terri, life seemed to take on a new freshness, much like the way the air feels after a heavy, cleansing rain. I laughed more than I ever had before, and I was already known for being a generally upbeat kind of guy. Of all her qualities I admired, it was her fearlessness that made me respect her the most. I had met optimistic people before, but never had I met someone so willing to put faith in the unknown.

It was this outlook that drove her to start her own pottery business with her brother and sister, out of nothing more than an urge to do something amazing. After completing all the research she could dig up, she began producing pieces for the local market.

Piling them all in her car, she'd drive from store to store, trying to introduce her beautiful pieces to mostly indifferent eyes.

"Perhaps another time," said one store's owner.

"They're nice, but I'm not sure my customers would want them," said another.

"The pieces are too big. Smaller would be better," said still another.

She pushed on for weeks and months, even having a long, loud cry one day on the fruitless drive home, her car heavy from the weight of wares no one seemed to want. And still she kept her eyes forward. She knew she had to keep going. If she could put enough faith out there, she said, then surely she'd be rewarded at some point. Then, just as she thought she might never see a dollar from her venture, she made her first sale. One store took every single piece. She was now in business.

"No, not without fear," she said one day when I asked about her positive approach to life. "It's more like in spite of it. I mean, what's the worst that can happen? You make a mistake? You mess it all up? Waste your time? Lose some money? Feel totally naked and vulnerable knowing that all the naysayers are probably having a good chuckle at your expense? No one wants that, of course. It's uncomfortable. And you do your best to avoid it. But when it does happen, then the kindest thing you can do is to forgive yourself if you feel that badly about it, and just move on. At least you can say you tried, and that's something to be proud of. Who hasn't blundered at one point or another in life? Or a few times, for that matter? Show me one person who's never made a mistake, and I'll show you someone who hasn't really shown up in their own life."

Terri was the daughter of a self-made businessman, who had started his wholesale liquor distribution business with just five cases of beer. She had watched her mother and him build it over the years into one of the largest of its kind in the Caribbean. She even worked in the business for some nine years before college. But her father left her mother and remarried when she was still very young. Her stepmother had never taken to her, had never been a nurturing adult in her life, and in fact was the source of some of the harder lessons she had to learn.

"Fear's the culprit," she said to me one day. "It affects our decisions, the way we think or behave, how we react to people and the issues they project on us. When you dig deep to the root of it, that's when you'll find fear. I may not have lived a lot of life. I may still be relatively young. But let me tell you, one thing I know for sure … that's no way to live."

I knew I was not about to let this remarkable woman slip through my fingers. I asked her to move in with me. She did. By Christmas, we were announcing our engagement. One night while planning and reminiscing, she confessed to suspecting that dear Fred may have used me as a chance to rid himself of a lemon of a tractor, as well as a troublesome worker whom he had wanted to sack for the longest time. I'll admit I was a bit surprised. It had taken me time and a fair amount of cash to get the tractor into good working condition—not exactly the deal I had expected. But, as our mutual acquaintance was the reason Terri and I met to begin with, we looked at it as life's way of collecting taxes on our latest and greatest reward—each other. So we decided that we'd still love Fred anyway. "Let's be grateful that it happened," she said. And we believed that to the core of our being. We had a good laugh over Fred and wished him God's blessings.

We got busy planning our wedding, which would take place in Ocho Rios at my small farm home. With family and friends coming in from around the globe, we had a lot on our plate and were enjoying every minute of it. Of course, I continued juggling my many business interests, some of which would take me to Kingston. On such occasions I'd visit the gambling club owned by a friend of mine. I admit that I had the gambler's blood in me. It was not something I was terribly proud of, but I thought of it as merely a form of entertainment, as well as a good lesson in human behavior. If you want to know something about people, see how they act when under pressure. Watch them lose at anything—a game, an argument, a bet, or even a relationship. Will they be nasty and bitter, or calm and accepting? Those are the colors of people you want to know.

That night when I popped in with Terri, I planned only on having a little fun with some friends. Terri had just become my fiancée when she accompanied me to the popular clandestine house for the first time.

It was not the evening I had expected. After making the rounds greeting friends, I settled down to a quick game of pai gow. As it began to turn in my favor, the blood rushed to my cheeks and my eyes twinkled like a kid's. But when my future wife saw the thrill on my face, hers grew sullen. She lowered her eyes and turned her head away. I asked what was wrong. That's when she started slipping her ring off. "I had a gambler for a father, Robert," she said quietly. "I love you, but I don't want a gambler for a husband. I can't do it. I just can't."

I grabbed her hand, curling it in mine, forcing the ring to stay on her finger. "No," I said looking into her eyes. Around us the shouts and bantering continued as patrons went about their evening of winning and losing. I did not want to leave a loser that night. I did not want to lose Terri. "Terri, if you want me to stop, I'll stop now. This means nothing to me. Nothing. You mean everything, honey. Please keep your ring on. Stay with me. Make your life with me."

If I didn't know it before, I knew it then. I wanted to be everything this woman expected in a husband. And if that meant changing or turning my back on a bad habit for a better one, then I was willing to do it ... because that's what love does. It challenges you to be your best, no matter how old or set in your ways you think you are. I kissed her on the cheek, and we never spoke about it again. I kept my word and never gambled after that.

On March 10, 1990, we officially became each other's life partner. That day, rain threatened to drench our afternoon outdoor reception, for which we had lined up not one, but two live bands, and a Tahitian dance number to be performed by my niece. With the stage, tables, chairs, and all the food and drink stations already in place, the decorators and I ran around frantically trying to salvage as much of the decoration and setup as possible under the intermittent deluge. Not thirty minutes before the first guests arrived, the rain clouds pulled back and made way for the most incredible afternoon tropical sun. Our wedding was beautiful and witnessed by over three hundred family and friends.

We made our home in Ocho Rios and began our life as a married couple. Our wedding was the first of a line of parties that we'd host at our home. Several would be huge, complete with live bands and the like. Motherhood came soon after we wed with our son Alex. Terri beamed with maternal joy at the life we had brought into this world, and became the kind of mother most could only hope to have. Justin made us a family of four a few years later. Terri wrote notes to her sons in a journal she kept, intending to hand it over when they became grown men. She joined any committee at school she could find just to stay involved. All homework and projects went through her. She was "mom on board" all the way.

Even after our sons, Alex and Justin, were born, my bride and I still acted as if we were teenagers stealing opportunities for passion behind our parents' backs—even though we were practically middle-aged and paying our own bills. Sometimes we stole private moments by the beach or river. We even got creative once on an ATV. We couldn't get enough of each other.

We snapped into place like two Legos. She owned and used a daily organizer and taught me how to streamline my workload and bring order to my day; I brought the spontaneity and adventurous spirit that had been missing in her life. "Honey, be sure to keep our passports in your purse," I'd tell her. "You never know when I may want to whisk my beautiful wife away to a romantic dinner in South Beach." And I often did. We lived in the "now," consciously present for every blessing that came our way—whether happy or sad—always with our eyes and hearts fixed on what was before us at that time.

As if sensing the pace that was right for us, we threw ourselves at our union with the urgency of star-crossed lovers. If we weren't equally skilled at a certain activity, we'd find a way to share the experience. Take, for instance, swimming. Terri was a weak swimmer who just managed to wade around. But with my help and encouragement, she sometimes came snorkeling just to be with me. The same went for running. Terri was not a runner, but she would wake up at 5:00 a.m. in the murky darkness and drive behind me as I covered my miles.

In those days, my obsession with fitness and the challenge of endurance got me running sometimes for as long as eighteen miles. I wanted to be stronger. Endure more. Push as hard as I could stand it. She carried my water and watched my back to make sure I wasn't mowed down in the dark by other vehicles. Once, some years before I met her, I was clipped on the shoulder by a motorist's side-view mirror. I went flying into the bushes, narrowly avoiding a messy death. Another inch and I'd have been instant roadkill. So I appreciated Terri's concern for my safety. I knew it had to be a boring experience for her—she could have just slept in or lounged while sipping her morning beverage—but she never complained once.

She even attempted alpine skiing one year on a trip we took to Vermont, although she thoroughly panicked and chewed my head off for accidentally taking us to the professional slope instead of the beginners'. We were so high up the mountain, that all we saw when we got off the lift was sky. We laughed the whole way down, much of which was done on our sore behinds. When we finally reached the end of the crazy slope, she playfully smacked me on the head and declared that I was still the only person on the planet who could convince her to do half of the insane things we did. "Robert, you're my drug. A couple doses of you and I feel I can do just about anything," she once told me. I could not have felt happier than if she had told me she loved me a hundred times a day.

The way we lived and loved one another—in practical terms— wasn't something we discussed or planned; we just went with what felt right. Even though much of our time was spent together, we each respected that the other was a separate individual with his or her own interests and dreams. We never attempted to crowd, clutch, or stifle each other with demands for time spent together that felt obligatory or measured. We treated one another like two birds with our cages wide open. We were free to fly as we wished on our own, all the while knowing that we would always return to our perch next to the other without feeling the threat of loss or abandonment.

But that was the foundation of our marriage: treasure the company of the other and allow room enough to *grow* in love after having fallen in love. As for arguments ... we had disagreements, of course, but we never allowed them to escalate beyond that. Somehow we had chosen subconsciously to be kind to one another and to put aside the need to prove ourselves right. It was not a new formula—we certainly did not claim to have cornered the market on marital success—but we put it into practice every day without fail. I can honestly say that we did not have a quarrel—a real one—in all the years we were married.

When it came to our hectic life, Terri became just as good a juggler as I was. One of our bigger moves was to rebrand her pottery business and take it to the next level. She was now set up with a larger studio I had built on my workshop compound. And so we were able to hire a handful of skilled artisans for increased, and more reliable, production.

Wassi is a word from old Jamaican dialect that means "terrific." In 1992, we rechristened her maiden venture as "Wassi Art" and reintroduced it to the local and tourist markets. This time Terri threw herself into even more technical research. It was a task she loved more than anything. If you wanted to gather information on something, you asked Terri. The glaze had to be compatible with the clay so that there was no crazing or leaking. Did we need to fire the clay more or less? What about silica? She located the best clay available on the island and made arrangements for its delivery. She investigated the international designer scene to learn which colors and patterns were coming out for the following year so that we could replicate them in our own designs and stay current. She accepted nothing that fell short on quality, and she constantly walked through the workshop talking with our artists, examining their work. "And our plates and mugs must be lead-free and microwave-safe," she insisted. "Wassi's pieces must be for everyday use as well as a source of happiness to the eye," she insisted. "It's the best or nothing."

We hit the hotel stores and soon filled their shelves with our colorful Caribbean creations. We even turned our studio into a tourist attraction, gladly hosting visitors interested in our work.

It didn't take long for us to start flooding both the local and the tourist markets with Terri's Caribbean-happy pottery.

Meanwhile, behind the scenes, I fell in love with so many of the bigger pieces, I'd pluck them out of the factory and take them home. Terri would always humor me and let me keep them for a short while before summarily returning them to the factory. "Unless we plan on turning our home into a gallery, I'm afraid these must go back," she would tease. "If we continue taking home the profits, we won't have a business!"

In those nascent years, we would spend our quiet moments laughing about archeologists two or three centuries in the future, unearthing our vibrant pieces with in-your-face Caribbean colors depicting how we lived and loved. We had no idea that what we had launched would become one of the region's most prolific producers of island pottery. It would only be a matter of years before Terri's Wassi Art pieces caught the attention of art enthusiasts, diplomats, and celebrities across the world, including the likes of Kofi Annan of the United Nations. I was not the least bit surprised. Terri had always been a passionate woman, driven by instinct and an inner strength beyond anything I had ever seen. I couldn't have been more proud to call her my wife, partner, and friend.

We were on a steady trajectory, and the wind was at our backs.

From Terri's Journal

May 19, 1991

My dearest Alexander,

This is the first entry of what I hope will become a childhood journal for you. Today is a Sunday. You are tossing and turning in your crib and teething with a slight fever. Dad and I are home with you ... At this time you already have six teeth and are standing very strong. You move about by holding on to everything you can grasp or by creeping. From your birth you've been an extremely strong child ... Whenever I take you from someone else, you hug me and put your head on my shoulder ...

You love the outdoors. Whenever you start to squirm and fuss, a walk outside always calms you down ... Dad has bought a backpack and you love it. Sometimes we go for long walks for miles.

June 20, 1991

On Father's Day you gave Dad a white Yaga cap. He loved it! You are now almost ready to walk. You are letting go of the furniture for longer periods of time ...

We took you to the zoo. You were fascinated by all the people. We all got soaked in the rain, which cut our visit short; however, we all had a good time ...

We can see you becoming more aware of your surroundings each day. You have now realized there are things above your head. You stare at the fans, light, trees, etc. We cannot take you outside now due to the mosquitoes. This frustrates you!

September 7, 1991

At this time you are very independent. Only you must feed yourself. Occasionally you allow us to hold your bottle. You have a very sweet temperament and go off to bed anywhere from 5:30

p.m. to 8:00 p.m., and sleep through to 6:00–7:00 a.m. You will awaken once or twice for juice, milk, or a diaper change. Once you have finished your bottle, you literally dive into the pillows.

October 1, 1991

Hello, Alex! You have enriched our lives beyond belief. Your dad is so proud of and happy with you. We look forward to coming home to you every evening.

October 29, 1991

Dad and I came in late two nights in a row now. You are already sleeping. We feel guilty (well, I feel bad about it because I'm not spending enough time with you). I have lost track of your teething. You now have approximately fourteen teeth, but no one can get to check it properly …

Life is good and happy at this time, although our cash flow is tight. We are hoping that we can find our way out of this soon.

May 17, 1992

Today you insisted on feeding me my bowl of cereal. It was so funny. You would lift the spoon to my mouth, and at the same time you would open yours wide to encourage me to eat up, and then you would do it each time saying "again!" Your aim is extremely straight! Whenever you throw anything, you never miss. Whoever's feeding you gets quite nervous. Lord help us if it's the wrong thing because we know it's coming back straight at us! We are all hoping you'll make a great quarterback.

August 20, 1995

Alex, you're almost five, and you've already learned how to swim! I'm so proud of you! You are swimming better than Mom. One morning, two days ago, as I was leaving for work, I looked everywhere but could not find my keys. You came and asked me to bathe and tidy you up, and so I did. Shortly after, I started searching for the keys again, and then you said, "Mommy, would you like me to help?" I said, "Okay!" And then you went directly to the china powder dish on the shelf in the living room, opened it, and handed me the car keys!

Sometimes even to live is an act of courage.

—Seneca

CHAPTER 3

Preparing for the Test

It was raining hard that Sunday, January 7, 1996, when I got the phone call that shook the foundation of my world for the very first time.

My watch said it was close to noon. I was in the middle of rearranging my day around the heavy showers, which made it dangerous to drive. With the island's roads already second-rate at best, it's the last place you want to be in a storm. It's an unwritten rule on the island that not much business gets done when Mother Nature's having a hissy fit. There's just no point.

I answered my phone by the third ring. My brother Pascal was at the other end of the line calling from Kingston, but I could barely hear him. The wind gusted outside, forcing me to ask him to repeat what he had said.

"Robert, Andrew's been in an accident! He's been in a car accident!"

"What?? How bad? Is he okay?" For a moment I heard nothing … and then came a deep, wrenching sob. I pressed the phone closer against my ear. "Pascal! Pascal, is he okay?"

"No … no."

Now trembling, I screamed into the phone, "What are you saying? What are you saying to me?"

"Robert, can you go to him now?"

Andrew was our younger brother. The accident had taken place not far from Ocho Rios. I was the only one who could get to him right away.

I only remember throwing myself into the driver's seat of my red Toyota pickup and making the pedal touch the floor. My foot tapped on the brakes only a handful of times. By the time I arrived at the hospital, my brother's body was already gone. They said it had already been taken to the morgue. I made my way there.

When I finally saw Andrew, his lifeless body was on the floor—the back of his head covered in sticky blood. That was the point of impact, the coroner told me sympathetically. Dead at thirty-four. The coroner assured me my brother hadn't suffered long, if at all.

My heart flew into my throat as I ran to him, screaming his name. "Andrew," I sobbed, holding his head in my lap. I started brushing his hair. "Wake up, Andrew, wake up! Please wake up! Don't die, brother, don't die!"

Before that day I had never seen death. I had never sat with it … had never really *been* with it outside of the setting of a funeral of an acquaintance or elderly family member. I'd only ever seen the body already fixed up and laid to rest respectfully in a neat box, while I sat close by in a fresh suit, singing carefully selected songs with family and friends in mourning. This time it was unfamiliar. This time it was raw. It was lonely. Terrifying. This time it was life knocked violently out of the body of someone I loved before I could even say good-bye. Before I could tell him what he meant to me.

I reacted to it with the fear of a small child and screamed again. I thought that I could scream so loud he'd wake up. I wailed and wept without a care as to who heard me. And then I lashed out. "Why, God? Why?"

I cried for what seemed like hours. My eyes began to burn, already stiff from the salt in my tears. My throat now hoarse, I trembled in silence, unable to say anything else. Then my mind began to wander, and that's when I started thinking about God. I sat there, almost in a trance. I don't remember much about the conversation I had with myself, or with God, but I can still feel the immediate calm that held me afloat as I sat there, alone, with my brother's lifeless body.

I must have asked "why" a hundred times over. Why now? Why my brother? Why did this have to happen? And what does it all mean? I had always thought that things happen for a reason, and I struggled now to make sense of my pain and my brother's untimely end. But this time the reason did not seem clear.

Eventually I was able to get up and walk to the adjoining office, where paperwork was waiting for my signature.

There is no question that I was reborn after Andrew's death. Terri, the boys, and I began going to church every Sunday. We had been raised in the Catholic faith but had never taken it very seriously. I admit that it may have been too obvious for us to turn to a higher power when we felt beleaguered, our backs up against a wall. But in the days and weeks that followed my brother's death, I was lost in a way I had never been before. The new day's sun, a challenging run, time spent with friends, music ... all simple things that once upon a time could easily toggle me into a happy mood, now had the effect of a placebo. Inside I was numb. I needed something to steady my soul. I needed to be propped up. I wanted to feel alive again.

We became members of Our Lady of Fatima Catholic Church. It was a simple but beautiful and inviting house of worship. Perched on the coastal cliff, it gave the congregation a partial view of the sea, and it had tropical louver windows that allowed the trade winds to steal through and cool our skin.

We embraced our new life in the same manner with which we approached everything—all of us, all in. Terri not only started teaching Sunday school, she also joined the choir. She even got me to sign up for it despite the fact that my singing was off-the-charts bad. "It's all about breathing," she said while coaching me. "So you may not be able to sing like a professional. But with a little practice you can do it, Robert. Everyone's got a voice just waiting for the right song."

That was typical Terri, always looking at life through happy eyes and seeing the best in everyone. We even began going door-to-door, evangelizing on behalf of our church. Many of our family and friends found the practice somewhat extreme. I'll admit that preaching—"Bible thumping," to be blunt—was out of character for me. I had always viewed religion as a more personal issue and not something to be shoved into people's faces.

But what wasn't unusual was our enthusiasm and dedication for whatever we believed in. It was the way we approached just about everything that was important to us. I did it for as long as it felt right. That's just how I was. If the vibe was there, touching me, prodding me, I'd respond.

A few months later, I woke up at the same time I always did, intending to start the day with my run. But for some reason— and I still can't quite say why—the air had a different feel about it. The sky was gray and overcast. Still in my bed, I could hear a light wind rustle through the palm trees outside my bedroom window ... not that that was unusual either. We had our share of bleak days. But somehow this one was different. I knew I would not run that morning. It just wasn't in me that day. But I still wanted to head for the sea. And so I waited.

When the time came to head down, I grabbed my float belt and walked out the door.

When I got to the beach, a now stronger, more unsettled wind was blowing about with an unusual chill. The morning sea greeted me with a restless, almost irritated stir. I have no idea why I didn't turn around and go back inside. I was a pretty strong swimmer, but I knew enough to never challenge the sea when it was in an uneasy mood. I always acknowledged and respected its power. If the sky wasn't blue and the current calm, I was not going in. Everything in my head told me to cancel my swim. Instead, I sat on the sand and stared out at as the waves crinkled and peaked, beckoning me ... almost challenging me. I asked myself why I was still there. Shouldn't I just go back home?

At some point I caught myself thinking about life—what it meant to be alive and to live. Then I thought about *my* life. I thought about some of the decisions I had made that I wasn't proud of, and what I wanted my life to look like now and in the future. I must have sat there for at least half an hour. Then, still in a state of meditation, I walked toward the water and sank into the coolness of it. It felt every bit as it looked—unpredictable. But I just kept going.

By the time I raised my head, the shoreline was a thin break in the distance. I turned to float on my back and stare at the sky. Above me, the lower clouds moved across the sky at a steady pace. A pair of seagulls drifted across on the wind, their wings fully outstretched. The sea rocked me as I breathed slowly. I allowed myself to trust where I was and the conditions around me. I gave a momentary thought to the dangers that might now be lurking beyond the safety of the reef. But before long, everything that I was fearful of disappeared. "I just want to be a good person," I said. "Please show me how." I'm not sure who was listening, or to whom or what I was addressing. Was it God? The universe? Me? I still don't know exactly. But in that wild sea that morning— alone, vulnerable, and searching—I sowed the seeds of my good intentions.

I must have been out there for at least an hour before I swam back to shore. The calm inside me completely belied the body of water from which I emerged. It was now even more restless. The only thing I was sure of at that moment was that I was going to make good on my promise. I had no idea that I was going to get the chance I had just asked for. The test of my life was already in the making.

From Terri's Journal

January 22, 1995

Welcome, baby Justin! We love you! You were born on Tuesday, November 22, 1994, at 5:35 p.m., and weighed a whopping eight pounds. You were a bit colicky for the first six weeks but have settled down now. As a matter of fact, you went to bed from 5:00 p.m. this afternoon. You love water, both to drink and bathe. You are cooing and gurgling and love to smile. You are trying to suck your fingers.

March 2, 1995

You started sucking your finger two days ago. You weigh sixteen pounds and are a very happy baby. You are laughing, cooing, gurgling, and trying to lift yourself up. Alex almost choked you today with your bib. You love when I dance you to sleep with music.

May 25, 1995

Your two front bottom teeth came out early May, and you are teething again. You eat well. Your favorite foods are banana with oats, and beef and vegetables. You still love water. You are like your dad—easygoing. Whenever you awake, you don't cry unless you are hungry. In the mornings you lie in your crib cooing and playing with your toys. In the nights after you've eaten, you want to be put down immediately. You will entertain yourself but don't like to be left alone.

June 14, 1995

Justin, you are so big! You love food. You grab at everything and eat anything. You try to wait up for us in the evenings. You're rolling everywhere and are almost ready to creep. You still laugh a lot.

September 13, 1995

Justin, you're a sweetheart. You are loving and will go to anyone who smiles with you. You'll go to complete strangers, put your head on their shoulders, hug and pat them ... Two more bottom teeth came out this week, so you now have six teeth. You love music! You dance to any little rhythm.

March 2, 1996

Justin (fifteen months), you weigh twenty-five pounds, three ounces, and you are thirty-two inches tall. Your favorite toys are keys and the telephone. You love to climb everywhere and anything. As soon as I get home at nights you want me to place you on the kitchen counter or to play with the water from the bathroom taps. As soon as I sit at the table to eat, you are there also.

It was only a sunny smile, and little it cost in the giving, but like morning light it scattered the night and made the day worth living.

—F. Scott Fitzgerald

CHAPTER 4

The Journey Is Heralded

By 1999, Wassi Art was about to step up to the next level with the opening of a new branch in Montego Bay. We had built our first website and established a product catalog. Meanwhile, Terri, the face and voice of the company, had also been given a spotlight on one of the island's popular morning talk radio shows. As the show's host began the interview, I listened with a proud smile. Terri's clear, eloquent voice came through the radio, speaking with poise and joy about the business she had literally started with her own hands. She sounded strong and youthful. In fact, I had never heard her sound more powerful than she did that morning.

On March 10, 2000, we celebrated our tenth anniversary by renewing our vows and hosting a reception at our home. Almost a month later, one of our young artists passed away. On the day of the funeral I had to be in Kingston on business, so Terri attended the service on our behalf; she would deliver one of the tributes. Standing before a packed church, she spoke about the life one of one so talented, and cut down so early.

And then it happened. She was returning to her seat when all of a sudden her right leg buckled, sending her to the floor. With the help of several arms that immediately reached down to grab her, she got back on her feet quickly. She took her seat in the pew, smiling graciously but still startled by the very public and unexpected fall.

Later that evening, she mentioned the incident as we ate dinner, almost as an afterthought. We had already almost finished eating our meal when she remembered to bring it up. "It was just so odd, Robert. One second I was perfectly fine, and then in the next, my leg just went out on me. Almost as if it had forgotten how to move."

"What do you mean, *forgot?*"

"I'm telling you. It failed me just like that."

"Did you feel any pain?"

"No pain."

"Weird sensation like numbness?"

"No."

"Some kind of tingling?"

"No, no tingling either."

I looked at her as if to give her more time to think about it. When she added nothing more, I nudged her again. "But you must have felt *something*, Terri. Your leg doesn't just stop working out of the blue."

"But that's just it! I felt nothing. It was the weirdest thing. It just went out like a light switch. I mean if I had to pinpoint a sensation at all, I would have to describe it as a sudden weakening of sorts just before it gave out on me. But that's about it, really."

"Okay, but how do you feel in general?"

"Just exhausted, I suppose, but that's nothing new. I've been feeling depleted for a while now. But I don't think it's more than what the average working parent goes through."

"We'll have Dr. Harper take a look at you. Make an appointment to see him as soon as we can."

"Oh, come on. I'm sure it's nothing, honey," she said, almost laughing at me. "I don't need to bother the doctor about this little thing." But I ignored her.

"No way, Terri. You're going. I'm taking you myself, so don't even bother to argue. And if you don't make the appointment, I'll do that too."

Terri nodded with an appreciative smile. "Okay, okay! I'll call him tomorrow."

"And in the meantime," I said with a grin, "maybe Dr. Rob should conduct a preliminary examination *tonight* to see if he can find that faulty switch!" We laughed and finished our meal.

A few days later we found ourselves at our family doctor's office. After what amounted to a ten-minute conversation, the good doctor pointed a finger at Terri's notoriously busy schedule and suggested that the culprit might be chronic fatigue syndrome. He also reminded her that at forty-three with two young children, she needed to pace herself better, maybe lighten her load a bit. Terri did admit to feeling generally tired. She smiled as she conceded that perhaps she had just finally piled too much on her plate. The doctor then prescribed rest and a B_{12} shot, which he administered right away. We left his office, with me teasing Terri about her now very sore butt, and both of us thinking that that was the last we'd see of the funny-leg incident.

In the last week of April, Wassi Art sent us to New Orleans for the city's annual jazz festival. Riding on the momentum of Wassi's growing success, we had accepted the invitation to showcase Wassi Art's pottery once again, as we had done before at the New Orleans Essence Music Festival. We couldn't stop smiling at the recognition of Wassi's work. We knew it would be a great opportunity to introduce our pottery to a wider audience and to have some fun at the same time. We couldn't wait to get packing. If there was one thing Terri and I loved doing together more than anything else, it was traveling.

We flew out of Miami. Two short hours later we arrived at the Louis Armstrong New Orleans International Airport. With our luggage in tow, we began walking toward our rental car, with Terri walking just a step ahead of me. She had one suitcase; I had the other.

We were within a yard of the vehicle when my wife began to stumble. This time I was there to grab her before she hit the pavement. Once she straightened up, we looked at one another. "Honey, what just happened? Did you trip on something?"

She gave me a slight smile but shook her head. "Ah, no. I think it's my leg again. Gave out like it did at the funeral."

"What? Do you want to go to the hospital? Are you feeling okay? Dizzy? Are you too tired?"

"No, Robert," she said, putting her hand on my shoulder. "I'm just fine, I promise. Look," she said, taking a few steps forward and back, "I'm walking with no problem now. See?"

When I protested, she assured me again that she was fine and laughed it off as old age sending her warning signals. "Some women get hot flashes; I get a malfunctioning leg! Come on, let's go," she said. "New Orleans is waiting for us! Let's not waste another moment on this silly thing."

For the first time I allowed a few seconds' worth of concern to seep in. *Exactly what was this mysterious leg problem?* But the moment didn't last. We were together in a beautiful city, and so we dashed aside all negative thinking. We immediately returned to our usual state of cheer and began hunting for a restaurant for some great gumbo. We completed our journey as planned, not allowing our unanswered questions to interfere. Why would we? Surely there was a logical explanation.

But this time it *was* different. Now there was a slight dragging of her right leg. But as it was barely noticeable, we didn't discuss it much, other than to pledge that once we returned home, we would investigate it further. In the end, the trip was a success, and New Orleans was everything we had hoped it would be.

Once we made our stop in Miami en route back to Jamaica, we asked Terri's brother Glen, a general practitioner, to help us order some preliminary tests. He immediately lined us up with a neurologist colleague of his. Dr. Sanchez ruled out cancer, much to our relief, but he agreed that it was not merely a pinched-nerve issue. In the end he gave us a presumptive diagnosis of tropical spastic paraparesis (TSP), a viral infection of the spinal cord usually found in the Caribbean and Africa. He referred us to the University of Miami for further testing just to be sure.

We did make an attempt to get an appointment, but there was none immediately available. With the big cancer ruled out, and no visible worsening of her leg, we decided to drop it and returned to Jamaica to see our boys. We were confident that the answer would come to us in its own time.

Some months later, Terri received a call from her sister Patty. She had, by then, left Jamaica with her husband to make a new life in Miami. They were doing well at their home-based export business, she said, but for some inexplicable reason she felt the need to switch careers and learn massage therapy. But there was a problem. Her husband was not happy with the idea. Their business was growing and needed her help. In addition, the marriage was on shaky ground. What did Terri think she should do?

Although always one to encourage others to follow their hearts, this time Terri took a different approach. She suggested that Patty stay true to her gut feelings but consider delaying her switch by a year or so. A delay would allow time for the business to grow, time for her husband to find help elsewhere, and time for their marriage to heal. But Patty responded with near desperation. "You don't understand," she said. "I feel that if I don't do this right now, I'm going to die!" In the end she would go on to become a certified massage therapist. Her marriage, however, would not make it.

Meanwhile, the boys' school year was coming to an end. Terri and I sat down one night and assessed our current situation. Our older son, Alex, was about to start middle school in the new semester. We felt this was a sign pointing to our next move, and we decided to make Miami our home base again. It had long been a second home, with family and friends on both sides already living there. The transition would be practically seamless for the boys. At the same time, we'd seize the opportunity to further investigate Terri's strange leg problem. With her brother there to help point us in the right direction, Miami felt like the place to be.

As a family we were excited about our new plans. Before leaving Jamaica, I began the process of lightening our load, and I made several trips to donate some used equipment from my printing house. I had decided that the equipment would go to Father Ramkissoon, a popular and hardworking priest who ran one of the island's larger skills training centers for youth. I knew that he would squeeze every ounce of good use out of the equipment. We then tied up loose ends for Wassi Art and left the factory manager in charge. With the flight to Miami a mere hour and a half long, the plan was that I would return at regular intervals to check in on things and keep our livelihood afloat. We were almost ready to go.

One day, with our departure date not far off, I happened to be in Kingston running through a list of last-minute errands, which included making a quick stop at the bank. While blessed with a unique vibe of its own, Kingston is a typical congested, busy island city, the part of the country most visitors tend not to visit, for reasons that are obvious. It has its issues. I remember feeling particularly irritated that day by the narrow, mostly potholed roads. The volume of traffic and pedestrians had long outgrown them.

Usually melting in oppressive heat, the city that day was sitting under a summer storm, courtesy of a tropical wave that was skimming by our south coast. It was the kind of tropical downpour that had the potential to turn roads into rivers, which was not hard when the city's gullies were perpetually clogged with garbage and debris.

It was starting to get ugly. I decided I'd run just one more errand before calling it quits for the day. As I was about to drive by the local YMCA, the traffic light switched to yellow. I stopped, deciding not to force my way through and possibly get stuck in the center of angry traffic. This happened to be one of the busiest intersections of all. Inside the cab of my pickup truck, I was cool and dry. Music kept me company through the radio. I hummed along while going through my list of remaining errands I'd have to put off for another day.

Suddenly, there was a light knock on my window. I turned to see the drenched face of a dreadlocked beggar. Being approached by a beggar was not unusual. This was a third-world island with many existing in different degrees of poverty. But there was something about his face—something in this man's eyes. This was no ordinary beggar. He was someone else. He looked at me as if he *knew* me. I felt that he could hear what I was thinking.

I held his gaze for a few seconds before blinking. Without even rolling the window down for fear of getting a little wet, I signaled with my hands going in a swift horizontal motion that I had "nothing" on me. It was a different version of a reply

I'd sometimes use if I didn't have any "small change" to offer. Technically I was being truthful. I had no small bills on me. But having just come from the bank, I had larger ones. Don't get me wrong—charity work had always been a part of my life. But that day, I'm ashamed to say, it wasn't a matter of generosity but convenience—or inconvenience.

He stood there, not moving away as I had hoped he would. That, too, was not unusual. Many of the vagrants were known to be quite aggressive, some to the point of being dangerous. They would often take it out on your car if they didn't get something, or enough.

But this fellow did nothing. He didn't argue, didn't gesticulate rudely, didn't curse. He locked eyes with mine. Suddenly, I began to feel conscious of every cell in my body, watching this withered man stand before me with the rain pouring down his face. He never once even tried to shield his eyes or wipe away the water that kept coming down.

After a few seconds, he then nodded and pulled away, his eyes softening with disappointment. I turned away, unsure of what had just happened.

The light switched to green and I sped off, feeling relieved. But within seconds of crossing the intersection, relief turned into embarrassment. Embarrassment into shame. Shame to disgust. What had I just done? Why hadn't I just given the man some money? I had more in my pocket right then and there than he'd see in a year.

As I continued down the road, my internal dialogue continued for a few minutes more. Of all the questions I asked myself at that moment, the one that kept sticking in my mind was this: *Why was I feeling this way? Why do I feel this heaviness in my stomach? Why do I feel so unworthy?* Be aware of what you're feeling, I'd always said. I had always preached that it was good to ask questions of one's self ... especially the hard ones. The trick was in the answer. It had to be an honest one.

Unable to get his face out of my mind and his hold off my conscience, I made a safe but unquestionably illegal U-turn and headed back to the busy intersection. I needed to find him.

It took me another ten minutes to get back to the intersection. When I finally got there, I parked across from the local YMCA and starting craning my neck in all directions, hoping to see him. I sat there for minutes, my eyes sifting through the pedestrians and other beggars who were crisscrossing the intersection. Nothing. And then, without warning, he appeared at my window. I rolled my window down and handed him a wad of money, but said nothing. He looked at me, gratitude seeping into his eyes. Then he began quoting me a Bible passage from the book of John. I let my conscience float on his words. In that moment I felt both forgiven and blessed. I nodded as he pulled back. Before I began to drive off, he had already disappeared again into the curtain of rain.

Life's challenges are not supposed to paralyze you;
they're supposed to help you discover who you are.

—Bernice Johnson Reagon

CHAPTER 5

We May Not Have Corner Vision, But We Still Drive

We arrived in Miami by midsummer. Not surprisingly, the city was soaking in its signature choking humidity, making us feel as if we'd been inhaled by one of the huge walruses at the nearby zoo. We got busy settling down in a modest home we had just bought south of the Kendall area. Terri was still complaining of general fatigue, so the boys and I encouraged her to rest, and we tried to do as much of the work as possible.

With the boys' schools, a supermarket, a pharmacy, a dry-cleaner, and other amenities all within a ten-minute drive of the house, we felt the location was perfect. Also convenient was the nearby Catholic church, which came highly recommended to us by a devout aunt of mine. Aunt June had, in fact, been actively encouraging me to take part in a retreat being planned for the following April 2001 in Jamaica, held by Father Ho Lung's Missionaries of the Poor. There was no question that I was interested. But having just relocated to our new Miami home, I was a little reluctant to spend more time away from Terri and the boys than was necessary. We wanted to start looking into Terri's health as soon as we could.

While she had not had a repeat episode of losing the leg's function entirely, the limp, which at first had been barely noticeable, was now becoming a part of her gait. And now, recently added to the list, was an odd but ever so slight twinge in her left shoulder that came close to rendering that limb temporarily unusable. "Pulled muscle" and "frozen shoulder syndrome" were among the first guesses. Both seemed fairly plausible, so her brother had X-rays taken to check her rotator cuff. Meanwhile, for good measure, Terri started chiropractic treatments with a doctor recommended by a friend.

By now her sister Patty was heavily steeped in her new career as a massage therapist, and she was thoroughly enjoying her new life. From the moment we arrived in Miami, she and her massage table had become regular fixtures at the house. She did her part in trying to care for her sister with a level of enthusiasm that was signature Patty. In that regard she and Terri were very much alike. If they were interested in something, 100 percent was the very minimum they were going to give. "Sister, am I ever happy I approved your career change," Terri joked during one of her sessions. "I mean, I knew you'd be amazing, but I didn't imagine I'd be one of your patients! I'm happy you listened to your heart!"

"Terri, it was the weirdest thing. I really felt as if I was going to stop breathing if I didn't make the change right then and there. Talk about strange, right?"

It wouldn't occur to Terri until years later that, somehow, the universe had already begun to put into place the people she would rely on the most for her long-term care.

This phase of massages, chiropractic care, tests, and X-rays continued into the following year. Still we found nothing. "We'll figure it out eventually," she said with a wave of her hand. It may be hard to believe, but up to this point we were not even close to losing even a night's sleep over this. That was about to change.

The worry started to itch at my skin the day her leg seized up on her while she was driving. As usual, I was making one of my quick jaunts back to Jamaica to check on Wassi Art. Terri had already pulled out of the Miami International Airport and was just entering the turnpike going southbound. Traffic was still fairly light at that hour. She was driving along, music playing from the radio, when suddenly her right leg went numb. She would later describe it to me as suddenly feeling as if her leg had simply vanished. Unable to engage the brake pedal, her heart pounding wildly against the wall of her chest, she quickly shifted in her seat and forced her left leg into position. She drove the entire way home like that—twisted in her seat, her sweaty palms glued to the steering wheel.

Her voice was still shaky when she told me about it over the phone a few hours later. I listened quietly as I pictured my wife in the terrifying situation, my own heart beating rapidly. I told her I'd take a cab on my way back in and that we'd get to the bottom of this. In the meantime, she was to keep her driving to a minimum, and avoid all highway routes until I returned, or ask someone in the family to help out. Once I got back, I made sure that Terri never had to get behind the steering wheel of a vehicle ever again.

Meanwhile, Aunt June kept at me about attending the upcoming Easter retreat. Her persistence didn't surprise me. What I didn't share with her, however, was that something inside was telling me that I needed to go. Whether it was a need for atonement or to make good on my promise to be a better person, I'm not sure. But what spooked me was that my aunt almost seemed to sense it.

The thought of participating in a religious retreat was not outside my radar. We had already been attending Mass as a family just about every Sunday. Terri did what she had always done and encouraged me to follow through if my heart said it felt right. At the time she was still walking fairly easily, although by now her limp was more noticeable. She *had* taken a fall one morning while trying to navigate around some boxes that were still in the way, but she assured me it was an innocent mistake. "I just didn't see where I was going and lost my balance," she insisted. Nevertheless, I used it as a reason to not go. "Listen, Robert. Do the retreat if it feels right. Don't worry about the boys or me," she said. "Alex and Justin will help in the house, and we'll be fine. Patty is close by, and I promise to take it easy. Just go. I'm so proud of you for doing this."

The retreat, held by a world ministry known to many, was not going to be an easy weekend of meditation and reflection under swaying coconut trees. We were expected to put our hands and hearts to work to help the poor and sick of the inner cities—the people that most run from and never see, or want to see. Our task would be to help feed them, talk to them, touch them, and even hug them. Many would be HIV/AIDS patients. It would be unlike anything I'd ever done.

A few months later, a small group of us touched down in Kingston at the Norman Manley International Airport. It was April. The persistent Easter winds saw to it that we had an extra-bumpy ride across the island's interior to the airport on the southeastern coast. But my mind was on the retreat. I admit that I was still agonizing over the fact that I would be physically interacting with those who were ill, or even facing death. Intellectually I knew I was not at risk for catching anything, but the fear stayed. It bothered me that I felt it. The last thing I wanted was to make the recipients of my care feel less than worthy; the very reason for the exercise was to make myself more worthy of serving them.

The following day we all gathered for a group introduction and prayer session at the beautiful mountaintop home of one of the coordinators. The purpose was to steel our resolve and soften our hearts before we set out to the inner cities to face the harsher realities of life.

It was, even by the island's standards, a beautiful morning. It was still early, and the air was fresh and lightly dewy. Above our heads, the new sun twinkled and smiled at us through the leaves of the huge pine trees. Beneath our feet, the dark-green grass shimmered. All around us, birds of different kinds sang their morning songs into the air, while a noisy woodpecker got busy making its presence known in its signature fashion. On the drive up the mountain Kingston looked quiet and peaceful. The deep natural harbor that sat south of it had also not yet awakened and looked like a mirror in the distance. It was a sight many of us had seen most of our lives. But so breathtaking was the vista before us, we all soaked it in as if seeing it for the very first time.

Kingston was, and still is to this day, regarded as one of the most dangerous cities in the world, with enough death by violence to rival that of an international war zone. Despite its troubles, however, our small group of twenty—all overseas Jamaicans—still loved the island we had once called home. Most of us had come from some level of privilege. For some, this was the first experience of its kind. None of us said it, but I doubt any of us had even driven our cars to the areas on which we were about to set foot.

As we got closer to our starting point, the scenes flashing past us began to deteriorate further and further. The heat began to intensify. We saw rusting zinc fences, barbed wires, listless beggars—some already picking through garbage piles ... distressed and frightened dogs that were mere skin and bones ... shoeless, shirtless young boys and men roaming aimlessly ... vendors of all ages selling their wares in makeshift kiosks ... While none of this was new to us, the intensity with which it came at us was. It made you go quiet inside. Very quiet.

The area we finally pulled into was worse than we could have imagined. The second we alighted from our vehicles, the heat and the stench of garbage and urine flew up into our nostrils like a mini-hurricane. I can only speak for myself, but I struggled to adjust to my new environs, already appreciative that it would be temporary, and already terribly ashamed for feeling that way.

Our first stop was at a home for the aged. It was a small building set in what is best described as a haven in the heart of the inner city. It was everything inside that the outside was not: clean, organized, and dignified. We walked into a somewhat cool but dark and sparsely furnished room. The smell of Dettol antiseptic and bleach greeted us before the residents knew we were there. Those who were able to get to their feet did so and greeted us with warm, often toothless smiles. Most, however, were wheelchair-bound or just too tired to do more than smile with their eyes.

As we made our way from resident to resident, I watched the Missionary of the Poor brothers embrace each sick elderly man and woman in the room, calling them by name. The residents smiled with each greeting, the gratitude for receiving care, time, and concern from another human being shining from their eyes. I started to relax somewhat. Not wasting time, we all settled in and helped to feed the residents, speaking with them if conversation was possible. I could feel the happiness flowing from them. Before leaving, we handed out the donations of clothing and other items we had gathered as part of our retreat exercise.

As we made our way to the next compound, I walked alongside one of the young brothers from India. Small in stature with a particular gentleness that made you unafraid to approach him, at only nineteen he had the look of peace and wisdom of one who had lived several lifetimes. It was as if he was an old man who had suited up that morning in the body of a much younger one. I knew there was not a single comment or any topic I could not put to him. So I posed the one question I was almost too embarrassed to ask, prefacing it with an apology. How, I asked him, was he able to touch and hold close to his face and body that of another who was so sick?

I will never forget his smile. It was warm, nonjudgmental, and almost approving. In fact, it was as if he had almost anticipated the question. I assumed at that point that it was not the first time he had been asked. "That's easy, Robert," he said, looking straight at me. "I see Jesus in everyone. The next person you come across could be Jesus. Remember that, and you will find helping another with unconditional love to be much easier. Remember that, and everything in your life will fall into place as it should."

At that point it occurred to me that if I could replace the faces of the strangers before me with the faces of the ones I loved, then I could find true compassion in my heart. So I did just that for the remainder of the retreat. I began to smile and touch with less hesitation. By the time we got to the AIDS babies, I was hugging tightly, and meaning it.

At the time I signed up for the retreat, I had viewed the exercise as a good offering, the conscientious act of a good citizen trying to be better, to do better. By the end of it, however, I understood that what I had just done was not unlike the challenges I had put my body through in the name of health and fitness. I now understood that only the challenge of in-your-face resistance could strengthen the soul. I didn't know it then, but I had turned a deeper corner in my journey.

Four days later, I boarded a plane and returned to my family.

If you have fear of some pain and suffering, you should examine whether there is anything you can do about it. If you can, there's no need to worry about it; if you cannot do anything, then there is also no need to worry about it.

—Dalai Lama XIV

CHAPTER 6

The Third Party in Our Marriage

In the months that followed my retreat with the Missionaries of the Poor, Terri's symptoms showed no signs of worsening. Still walking with relative stability, she had not had a repeat incident of the leg giving out entirely on her. We took that as a positive sign and allowed ourselves to forget about it, moving on with our lives, our focus now on our boys.

That period of temporary calm changed in early 2002, however, when Terri began to start dropping things. At first it was a mug, a book, the remote control—nothing of any significant weight or size. We thought little of it. Then one day she had another fall. This time it happened while she was going up the stairs carrying the laundry to our rooms. Again she fell on her left shoulder, the side that had already been giving her some problems. But now she was complaining of a weakness in the entire arm itself. She had trouble moving it even for simple chores. We called her brother Glen, who immediately made arrangements for her to see the same neurologist she had seen two years before. This time, he said, we'd delve further.

The doctor greeted us like family and gave us his undivided attention. We relaxed, knowing that we were in good hands once again. After he gathered the preliminary information, he suggested that the next course of action should involve a series of more intense tests. Terri would do the more basic ones as an outpatient, and then she would stay for a couple days and nights at the hospital so they could run numerous more sophisticated tests, and observe her closely.

At this point I should mention that there is no actual test to determine the presence of ALS. All a doctor can do is go through the process of elimination. It promised to be a tedious and expensive process, as all the usual suspects had to be addressed, including the big ones like multiple sclerosis and Parkinson's. We were anxious but not in a negative way. We were happy to be finally getting to the bottom of the funny leg mystery. Unbeknownst to me, however, Terri had already taken to doing her own research on the Internet for several weeks now. She had not shared her findings with me or anyone else, not even in passing.

We pulled up to the Baptist Health Homestead Hospital on a Wednesday. Above us, the rain clouds that had been gathering off the coastline to the east that morning were now moving inland. We took our time circling the parking lot before finding a spot not far from the entrance. "Okay, honey, let's do this," I said with a pat on her leg.

We walked into the cool air-conditioned lobby and soaked in the immediate relief it offered from the already muggy day. We were both in high spirits, and we talked and smiled like two people assuming that good news was already on its way. We felt certain that in a matter of a day or two we'd be given the name of the mystery ailment, and a set of prescriptions to hand over to the pharmacist so that Terri could start taking whatever medication it was that would set her on the path to recovery.

Meanwhile, I decided that I would sell the house and look for a single-story home. I knew I was acting on impulse again, but I felt it was the right thing to do for Terri. While she checked in and went through the requisite paperwork, I called our realtor and asked her to start working on it right away. I didn't want my wife falling down any more damn stairs.

We got settled in as the nurses had her change into her hospital gown and gave her the usual orientation talk. When the nurses saw me lingering, I let them know that I'd planned to be there for as many of Terri's tests as I could. I'd only leave to pick up the kids from school and then later on once visiting hours were over.

If Terri was nervous about any of the tests she was about to endure, she didn't show it. We chatted and laughed as we always did about whatever nonsense it was we were discussing. She called the boys that night, ordering them to do homework and get to their beds so they'd be rested for school in the morning.

The tests began the following day. For the most part, they were bearable. Terri sailed through the PET scan, nuclear scan, blood tests, urine tests, and electrical impulse tests. The spinal tap extraction, however, was another story. The sight of what seemed to be a foot-long needle was enough to make me break into a cold, damp sweat. I swallowed nervously. They numbed her skin in preparation, although it seemed like an unbelievably insignificant gesture for such an aggressive assault on her body. Before he proceeded, the doctor warned Terri that any movement on her part could lead to disaster. She threw me a quick brave smile before forcing herself to go rigid. I held her left hand and shoulder while the nurse held her right. I wanted to hold my own breath out of sheer fright but smiled instead and told her she'd be just fine. I admit to shutting my eyes when the needle began to disappear into Terri's spine. I couldn't watch. All the while she squeezed my hand. We both exhaled openly when it was over.

"That's the worst of it now, honey," I said. "You can relax now."
"And so can you!" she replied, grimacing.

Two mornings later, the tests behind us, I returned to the hospital to bring Terri home. I went past the nurses' station and smiled, the door to her room now in sight. As soon as I was about to push her door open, I did an exaggerated reggae bounce and walked in with a smile.

"And how's my beautiful wife this morning?"

Terri was alone in the room. Still in her bed, she was in tears, her eyes visibly red and swollen from where I stood at the doorway. The smile I had been wearing immediately switched to a frown. Within three or four hurried steps I was by her side, my keys and cell phone already thrown onto the visitor's chair. I leaned in and clasped her shoulders with my hands.

"Honey? Honey, what is it? Why are you crying?" Terri closed her eyes and shook her head. Trembling, she struggled to take a couple deep breaths before opening them again.

"ALS. It's ALS." For a few seconds I said nothing as I stared at her weeping, trying to remember the last time I saw my normally cheerful wife shed even a single tear. I had never heard of any such illness. I searched my mind for some modicum of recognition.

"Okay ... ALS ... well, what *is* it? Is it that bad? I mean, we can fix it, can't we?" Terri shook her head and covered her face with her hands. I pressed on, the frown on my face deepening. "Honey ... honey, please talk to me. What is this thing? What's ALS?"

"Lou Gehrig's disease. It's a ... terr ... terrible neurological disease." She stifled a sob and wiped her eyes. "The worst there is."

I grabbed the box of facial tissues and yanked out a couple for her. My face was still frozen in a frown. "Okay, but surely there's a cure? Medication? An operation? Some kind of procedure?"

"No ... no cure." I felt my throat constrict. I could barely swallow before asking the next question.

"Terri. Terri, honey, what do you mean there's no known cure? This is the twenty-first century! Doctors can even cure cancer in some cases! Honey, what are you trying to say to me?" Now she looked up into my eyes and held her gaze. I saw a fear in them that I had never seen before. This time her words came out in a hurt, strained whisper.

"I'm saying that it's ... it's terminal. That I will most likely die in two to five years. That's the average life expectancy for someone with this disease. I'm saying that my life will end ... in slow ... suffocation."

I remember her saying more. I know she said more. I can still hear her voice trembling as she tried to explain what she knew. But I had already stopped listening at the word *terminal*.

The room began to spin. I sat on the edge of the bed, my breathing becoming shallow as my heart started racing. I stared at her, still not really hearing what she was saying. The questions started coming at me:

Why was this happening to us? The love of my life ... she was only forty-five years old! How could she be dying already? Where did this disease come from? Why a disease with no cure? Why my precious Terri?

No answers came. After a minute, I willed my attention back into my body and to my tearful wife.

"But, Terri, are they sure? Are the doctors absolutely sure, or are they still searching?"

That's when she told me that earlier that morning, she had overheard Glen and the neurologist discussing the results while in the room. They had been careful to keep their voices down, but they didn't realize that Terri could still hear, or that she would even understand what they were saying. Not only could she hear, she recognized the name *ALS* from her own research and immediately began crying. They had tried to console her, of course, but the deed had already been done.

I pressed her on what was said, exactly.

"He said he only 'thinks' it's ALS ... but," she lapsed into a heavy sob, "I could tell by his tone ... that ... oh, my God, that he's sure of it."

This time the tears poured from me. I put my arms around my wife and held her tight, rocking her the entire time. She shook in my arms like a frightened stray as we cried together, my face buried in her hair, my eyes shut tight like they would never open again. We clung to one another for several minutes before I found the strength to pull myself away. I looked at her. The tears continued to stream down her face, and I reached for more tissues. I wiped her face slowly and then turned to my own.

That's when I decided I couldn't let Terri see me frightened like this. I couldn't let that happen. She needed to see me react the way we had always tried to—with epic optimism. Especially now. I steadied my voice.

"Honey, listen to me. Look at my face. We'll beat this," I said, still wiping her tears away. "Come on, honey, you know how we are! We can do anything we set our minds to. You know this about us."

"Robert—"

"No. We'll get another opinion. Doctors are incredible! They save lives! But they can be wrong too. Isn't that right?"

She shrugged. "Yes, but—"

"No! No 'buts.' This doesn't end here, Terri. We started out thinking it was chronic fatigue syndrome, and that diagnosis was wrong. We thought it was a bunch of other things, but they all turned out to be negative. This could be wrong too. Why not? It's possible. It's only a process of elimination that's brought them to this conclusion. We're going to seek another opinion. Don't cry another tear, honey. We're going to beat this ... this *thing*, whatever it is. I love you. Come on, now. Let me see you smile."

And with that, Terri managed to halt the flow of her tears. Maybe it was just a huge lie that only love could conjure up, but I needed to see her smile because hers could make everything bad go away. And she did it—for me.

Before we left, the doctor spoke with us. This time he gave us both the official results. After explaining to us what we could expect down the road as the disease progressed, he suggested that we look into professional care. He then wished us well. I have to admit that try as he did, I didn't see much hope in his eyes. We thanked him and told him of our plans to seek a second opinion. He was kind enough to give us the name of Miami's top neurologist, a Dr. Walter Bradley of the University of Miami's ALS center. He had written several books on the disease, he told us. The wait would be long, but if we wanted the top name in the field, then he was the one.

We then stopped at Glen's office across from the hospital. Glen did his best, as he wore both hats that day—brother and doctor—and told us he'd be there to support Terri and me in any way he could. He also gave Terri a prescription for antidepressants.

It's a strange phenomenon, but facing the world after you've been given bad news suddenly makes you acutely aware of your surroundings. When we finally emerged from the hospital and started walking to our car, the sun, now past its peak for the day, was warm and kind on our faces. It felt comforting, like an unexpected caress. And yet it stood in stark contrast with the storm that was raging in our hearts. It made Terri's diagnosis seem all the more cruel.

By the time we pulled out of the hospital's parking lot, Terri had already stopped crying. She was still shaky but managed a comment on how excited she was to be going home to the boys. I was not surprised. To wallow in sadness was as foreign a concept to her as remaining seated while music was being played. It simply was not in her genetic makeup. Instead, in as calm a voice as she could muster, she began telling me everything she had learned in her research about this dreaded disease. She came at me with stages, symptoms, and the inner workings of a mysterious illness that still seemed to have the medical community in search of answers. While trying to navigate the challenging Miami traffic, I listened carefully as my wife began to take charge of her life.

Beyond coming up to speed with the diagnosis, we agreed that we would not tell our children anything yet. It didn't make sense scaring them, and we still wanted to get that second opinion. All they knew was that Mom's leg and shoulder had gone weird on her. That the problem could be something that would take her away from them forever did not even appear on their radar, and we weren't about to place it there. Perhaps it was unfair of us to keep them in the dark. Terri was, after all, their mother. But we felt that they were too young to handle something so unbearable ... so ugly ... so frightening. We decided at that point to keep it from them for as long as we could.

When we finally drew close to our home, I reached over and squeezed Terri's hand. I admit I was looking for another one of her smiles to help calm me. As if reading my mind, she turned and sent one my way. Maybe it wasn't her most sincere smile, but she put her greatest effort behind it.

At that moment, ALS became the third party in our marriage. As frightened and unprepared as we were, we did the only thing we could. We made room for it and assumed our roles as gracious hosts.

We cannot direct the wind, but we can adjust the sails."

—Thomas S. Monson

CHAPTER 7

When Life Dumps Fertilizer
on You, You Grow

We didn't wait for the dust to settle after the initial diagnosis. We returned to our normal routine as husband, wife, and parents as best we could. In private, Terri and I acknowledged the elephant in the room, but we chose to not be outwardly jumpy about it. Instead, we took action and immediately set about securing an appointment with this Dr. Walter Bradley. It was a good thing we had been warned about the unusually long wait. The next available appointment with the good doctor was not until December. We grabbed it and began working on an interim plan of action. Soon we secured an earlier appointment in September with the ALS clinic at the Mayo Clinic in Jacksonville. All we had to do now was wait. And live. In hindsight, our stage of denial had begun.

Meanwhile, life had also been moving along at its own clip, with no consideration for the fact that the red flag had just gone up warning of rough seas ahead. In our absence, our main business in Jamaica had gone flat and was showing signs of worsening. But with the island's economy as bad as it was, complicated by the fact that the search for Terri's correct diagnosis now forced us to remain more in the United States, we could see that our beloved Wassi Art was about to go through its own bout of poor health. Not yet armed with all the answers, we decided on a family summer holiday in Jamaica so we could try to shake off our blues a little, clear our minds, and see what could be done about reviving our livelihood. By now the file we had made in our home office labeled "Medical Bills" was getting thicker. Terri and I agreed that perhaps it was time to put our assets to work for us. We would have to start the process of liquidation.

We jumped on a plane for the short flight to Jamaica the week the boys were out on summer holiday. As the aircraft positioned itself to land at the airport in Montego Bay, we drank in the vista of the blue sea and familiar sugar-white coastline; it was like medicine for a weary soul. Within a couple hours after landing, we pulled into Ocho Rios and into the driveway of our old home.

Starting the very next day, we threw ourselves at all our familiar beaches and eateries, saw friends and family, and fell back into the life and culture that had been our foundation as a young family. Terri and I cloaked ourselves with the warmth of old familiar faces. Deep down, we needed a distraction from the fact that her limp was persisting and that her arm had not regained its strength. Walking, even standing, now seemed a not-so-easy task for her. I stayed as close as I could to my wife and asked our house staff to do the same whenever I had to leave. Eventually we got her a walking cane. As much as we appreciated the sense of security the cane gave Terri, I admit we also felt somehow that we were giving in to whatever it was that was taking over her body.

Terri and I continued to live off the hope that the diagnosis was completely wrong, and that the culprit was nothing quite so sinister. Whether it was the right thing to do or not, we didn't share the doctor's diagnosis with our friends or family on my side. Naturally, anyone with eyes could tell that something was wrong.

It wasn't that we wanted to fool them or keep them out of our lives. We just didn't want to give the truth more muscle than we had to at this point. So we met their questions with a smile and assurance that we were still looking into it—it was the diluted version of the truth.

One of the beliefs Terri held was that if you say something, be it good or bad, you put the intention out there. To talk about her illness would be to encourage the negative thoughts, she said. And thoughts often led to manifestation. So she'd be damned if she was going to manifest or encourage anything that didn't lead her to health and happiness. I followed her example and turned my attention to the matter of the family's income. I told myself not to worry, that I'd fix it. And so I maintained a calm both inside and out.

A couple weeks later, still in Jamaica, I spoke with a former business partner who had also recently emigrated to the United States. He was now living in the Miami area, where he had just established a new company. Editscope, Inc., he said, dealt with digital editing of films and videos, using cutting-edge technology. As I was drawn to anything that involved the creative, it wasn't long before our casual conversation turned into an impromptu business meeting. My associate was a bright and talented individual, and he had the added advantage of youth's energy in his favor. An hour later we had a gentlemen's agreement: Terri and I would become partners in this new venture.

I admit it was impulsive, but I thought the business had potential and would bring something positive to our lives. My second reason for agreeing to the venture was for Terri. I felt that having something to focus on, to occupy our minds while we worked on getting her the correct diagnosis and treatment, would be a plus. We had always kept up a lively tempo in our lives, and I felt that some semblance of normalcy would be good for her ...

and me. I even suggested that we take a course on how to build websites just to get our feet wet in the business. We'd put our creativity to work. She liked the idea immediately.

Not long after that, we got a call from our realtor in Miami. She had found a buyer for our house. Did we want to proceed with the sale? I admit we were surprised. The house had been on the market for only a couple of months. Naturally, I turned to my wife for her opinion. Terri agreed we should accept the offer.

That night we shared the news with the boys. After being in our house for just about one year, we were now homeless. A surprise state of limbo, we called it. We all decided it would be a new adventure for the family.

Life is short, live it.

Love is rare, grab it.

Anger is bad, dump it.

Fear is awful, face it.

Memories are sweet, cherish it.

—Author unknown

CHAPTER 8

Our New Normal

Patty generously offered us her spare bedroom to squat in until we found a new place. Immediately upon returning to Miami, we rented a storage container and shoved everything in there, save for one suitcase each of clothing. As the four of us would be sharing a small bedroom, there would be no space for anything that wasn't absolutely necessary. As grateful as we were for the bridge of support, we knew it was just a matter of time before the cramped living space would wear on the family, as would the imposition on Patty. We'd need to find a new home soon. Meanwhile, Terri had "graduated" to a walker. The disease was progressing. Still, we refused to accept that it was anything serious. We were practicing positive thinking ... total mind power. Terri would have it no other way.

One day, while driving around in the Hammocks community just minutes away from Patty's home, I saw a rental sign for a two-bedroom apartment on the ground floor. The location was perfect. It was but a stone's throw from a beautiful lake, and a shopping plaza that had a great video game arcade center the kids would love. In my heart I knew it was exactly what we needed. I called Terri literally as I was making my way to the property manager's office. Within two weeks we were moving into our new home.

With just our essential belongings, we immediately threw ourselves at the tiny two-bedroom abode with the thrill of holiday campers. It was the smallest place we had ever called "home," and yet our spirits took to it immediately. We settled into our new routine and embraced it with sincere happiness.

Each morning I'd make breakfast for the family, take the kids to school, return home, and help Terri get dressed. Then we'd head up to the Design District by Miami Beach to spend a few hours each day at the offices of Editscope. We had already made good on our threat to take a course together on constructing websites, and we were eager to learn as much as we could in our new venture without interfering with the work already in progress. Terri had taken over the bookkeeping responsibilities, while I busied myself with the customer side of things, along with my partner.

By now I had gotten Terri a wheelchair. She still had enough strength in her arms to use a walker, but the wheelchair proved convenient when we needed to move faster. And as we were in the cosmopolitan part of Miami, we'd often treat ourselves to a romantic lunch at some of the area's trendy restaurants. Terry would carry our briefcase on her lap as I wheeled her through the conveniently flat city streets. Honestly, had I been a bystander observing us, wheelchair aside, I'd have thought I was looking at a couple with not a worry in the world. Later in the afternoon, we'd pick the kids up from school. While I looked about dinner, Terri would be monitoring the boys' homework, a task that had always been hers. They were fairly strong students, but Terri liked to stay on top of their school life. I ended each evening by giving her a bath and washing her hair. And on weekends, we continued to attend Sunday Mass faithfully. By now we had the congregation praying for us, at times literally over us with hands outstretched, praying for an answer to whatever it was that had gripped Terri's body, and a return to our life as we once knew it.

Even up to this point the boys had not asked us directly what was going on with their mom. We assumed the lack of questions meant that they were okay. Looking back, I now understand that we were wrong in our assumption. As subtle as they were, the signs were indeed there. Justin, our younger son, had become quieter than usual, not engaging us in conversation unless he had to. Meanwhile, Alex had begun spending increasingly longer periods at the nearby arcade, and he was showing signs of moodiness. The introduction of the wheelchair didn't make things easier. The boys understood that their mom was getting sicker, but still we never discussed it. Perhaps they resented us for keeping it from them, but we didn't want to scare them. And we certainly didn't want them jumping on the Internet to research ALS and find out the horrible truth.

In hindsight, we should have anticipated the uneasiness they had over their mom's condition. At first I'd take Terri to PTA and other school functions and meetings like we used to in the past, only this time in the wheelchair. But, more and more, we noticed the boys finding excuses to move away from us as soon as we'd arrive. At first we thought they just wanted to be with their friends, as is usually the case with kids. But we soon figured out that it had nothing to do with that at all. So we decided to avoid putting them in that situation altogether. Terri stopped attending all school functions from that point on. If she was hurt, she didn't show it.

It wasn't that I was embarrassed about Mom. She was my mom and I loved her. But I was at that age when you just want your parents to blend in like the wall, you know? You want them to be "normal" like every other parent. You cringe if they even wear, say, or do anything remotely odd. So whenever she'd come to school in the wheelchair … yes, I felt uneasy. I felt guilty about feeling that way, but it's the truth. The thing is, I didn't know she was dying. I knew she was sick, and getting worse. But dying? No. Maybe I'd have reacted differently had we been told the truth. No way to know for sure. Now that I'm a little older, I understand that my parents were trying to protect Justin and me. It made sense, I suppose, to keep us in the dark like they did. We were way too young to deal with it. And they were still hoping for a miracle, I guess … not just for Mom but for all of us. I don't how else to put it … sometimes I felt as if we were growing up without parents. They were physically there, making sure we were taken care of and all, but at the same time they seemed so mentally and emotionally distracted by what was happening. After a while I began to hate whatever it was that had Mom stuck in that wheelchair. I just hated it.

—Alex

I was too young when Mom first became sick to understand what was going on, or to even feel scared. I just did what kids do—I adapted with each phase she went through. First the limping, then the cane, then the walker. I got used to each one. But when they finally got the wheelchair, that's when I sort of held my breath and widened my eyes. It looked so menacing. And permanent. But I didn't ask my parents anything. They told me Mom was sick, and that was all I knew. But what I understood for sure was that we were no longer like other families. Now Mom and Dad were less involved in school activities.

I suppose that upset me a little, even though I understood that sometimes they just couldn't handle it and weren't being lazy and making excuses. I wouldn't say I was an unhappy kid. I never once felt uneasy about coming through the front door. I never felt as if I wanted to be anywhere else but home. I still talked with my mom, even when years later it became hard to understand her. I'd still sit beside her and just talk. I could always tell when she was trying to be cheerful for me. As for my dad ... he had always been a strong man in my eyes, but I never saw him stronger than when Mom became weak. I was proud of him. I knew that he was giving up a lot in order to take care of her. And it was obvious that he did very little for himself. So whenever I found myself feeling upset—resentful—I told myself that there was nothing any of us could do but love them.

—Justin

It is my regret to this day that we didn't address their unspoken questions. Perhaps we didn't have the energy to; maybe we were too afraid ... but they were our children, our responsibility, and we were acting on instinct to protect them. But to this day, I still wonder if in the long run they would have been better off knowing the truth.

We continued with our routine and did our best to stick together. Whenever there was an activity we could enjoy as a "normal" family, like taking in a movie or going out to dinner and visiting with family and friends, we did it. Whenever the weather was pleasant, we'd all head for the lake so we could run around for exercise, with me pushing Terri in her wheelchair. The lake was a beautiful escape that allowed us to temporarily break free from what had become our new normal. I suppose there was just something about being outdoors, working up a good sweat, laughing, and allowing ourselves to be distracted by the other residents who had also come to take refuge by its shores. It was at times like these when we would see the boys really let their shoulders relax.

By now necessity had become my inspiration, and I took over the running of the household. Terri, of course, remained by my side and still more or less at the controls. Never a heavyweight in organizational skills, I suddenly found myself moving about with an increased focus, taking care of the cleaning, laundry, and even the cooking. As a typical Jamaican man who had lived a pampered life of 'round-the-clock help, I knew only how to boil water to make coffee. Before, if I wanted fresh clothes, I needed only to open my closet and reach for something already cleaned and ironed.

Terri taught me how to feed our family and look after our home life. She started by giving me the grocery list each week. Once I returned with the items we needed, she'd sit in a chair by the kitchen and dish out step-by-step instructions on how to prepare this meat, and how to cut up that vegetable. She'd give specific measurements and instructions on how high or low the burner needed to be, how fast or slow to stir, when to cover or uncover—she gave every detail as only Terri could. I followed each instruction carefully, not daring to venture off by even a fraction. I'd line up all my measuring spoons, set the necessary ingredients on the counter, measure them out one by one, sticking to the letter of the recipe. Through Terri, I learned all our family favorites, including many Jamaican and Chinese dishes that we just had to have at our dinner table.

Before long I began to see the kitchen as an extension of my new life. I began cooking without fear, eagerly planning meals, eyeballing the measurements, and relying instead on the best ingredient of all—instinct. So far no one had become ill, and for that alone I was encouraged. One day, I happened across an infomercial about a cooking product called Set It and Forget It. "That's for me!" I said, and I immediately ordered one. The meals I produced from that were actually tasty, which encouraged me to start inviting our office staff over for dinners on occasion. To see other people eating my food and loving it was a thrill I had never experienced before.

My next adventure was sushi. I bought the kit, experimented, and even took a sushi lunch to work for everyone, chopsticks and all. Terri teased that I went from zero to sushi in a matter of weeks. We were having our own brand of fun in that little apartment, experiencing a certain kind of joy in having to redefine our family dynamics. I found the feeling of self-sufficiency refreshing. "Change" is my middle name, I have always said. Indeed, I had always viewed new situations as exciting, even if intellectually I knew they were downright scary. And I did so now with a smile. The way I saw it, there wasn't much else to do but chin up and move forward.

By this time, Terri was becoming more and more dependent on my help for some of the basic functions. These included some of the more private ones, of course, such as going to the bathroom. With her arms growing weaker, she could no longer coordinate herself effectively to get the job done. So we bought a special bottle used by hospitals that allows patients to stand and relieve themselves. I'd say we made the transition with relative ease. Yes, I'll admit that the first time I had to clean her up, there was a little nervous laughter between us. She joked that all her attempts to maintain some degree of mystique as my wife had now most certainly gone down the proverbial drain. I simply replied by kissing her on the cheek, and telling her that I was honored and blessed to be given the chance to get to know her like I never had before.

Meanwhile, Terri continued to be her own village doctor. A little research had led her to a clinic in the Kendall area that did hair testing as a way to measure one's nutrition levels. We promptly made an appointment to have her checked out. Her results surprised us. According to the results, she was malnourished.

"You're what?" I said with surprise. "Malnourished? But we eat so well! How can this be?" And that's when she explained the harm that microwaving and eating processed foods can do.

"It's okay, honey. This we can fix right away," she said. "We'll all get healthy, starting now. It's all about holistic living."

After we received the test results, she was put on a nutrition program personally designed for her blood type. It was similar to the Atkins diet and included megadoses of vitamins. She added to this weekly acupuncture treatments and Chinese herbs in pill form, as well as back machine massages. Her holistic doctor also introduced her to silver as a healing mineral and suggested she consider a hydrocolonic cleansing.

"Silver?" I said, a little baffled. "Isn't that something you wear? Since when did silver have healing properties?" I admit that this new world of holistic medicine was completely foreign to me. Before ALS, Terri knew little about it. And I, even less.

Her thinking was that she'd fight ALS, or whatever was attacking her, with the best weapon she could offer: a body that was as toxin-free as could be. I wasn't a research kind of guy, so I just encouraged her to go with whatever made her feel proactive. In fact, I encouraged her to do anything that made her smile with hope. After more Internet research one day, she announced that her first step would be to remove all the mercury fillings she had. "Mercury's toxic," she said. "If we don't want it in our foods or hospitals, then why do we have it in our mouths? I've got to get it out of my body!" We jumped on it right away and got our dentist to change her fillings so she could be mercury-free.

We monitored Terri, watching for any signs of improvement. At first I thought it would be like watching an orchid bloom. We were bound to see a gradual change. But it was more like watching grass grow during the dry season. Eventually she admitted that while she felt a bit more energetic, and her legs felt somewhat softer and warmer to the touch, the improvements were subtle and short-lived. I heard the faintest sound of disappointment in her tone. Disappointment but not defeat. "We'll keep trying, honey," I told her. "Don't give up."

One night I decided to cook a salmon meal. Again we invited the Editscope family over to join us. They came and devoured my work, singing my praises for being a pretty decent cook. That's when my wife turned to them. "And do you know why this meal tastes so good?" she asked. "It's because Robert prepared it using the most important ingredient of all … love."

And with those words, my beloved Terri refilled my tank. Nothing I ever did for her was considered a chore. But knowing that I was truly appreciated was all the fuel I needed. In fact, it made me want to do even more.

When the twin towers in New York City came down on that fateful morning of September 11, 2001, we watched in horror as we got ready for our daily stint at Editscope. We could not have known at that moment that the tragedy would become another indirect blow to our lives. Our business, like so many others, would suffer in the months and years to come as a result of the attack.

We soldiered on and made our daily treks to the office. We relaxed in the distraction of light work and socializing that the little company brought us. By now Terri's speech was sounding slurred. She described it as navigating the words around a lazy, heavy tongue. "Like it's falling asleep!" she said. I joked that if I didn't know her better, I'd have to assume that she was indulging in too many afternoon cocktails. We tried not to worry. Our Mayo Clinic appointment was approaching fast. Then we would have the right answers. We'd be on our way to fixing the problem.

In response to the deterioration in her speech, Terri decided to tweak her diet again, this time to organic foods. The change signaled her move to an even deeper holistic way of living. Once again she jumped on the Internet and began researching.

Weeks later, it came time to make the seven-hour-long drive to Jacksonville in our minivan. We grabbed some of our favorite CDs and packed the wheelchair and a couple of overnight bags, along with a lot of hope. We were now just days away from D-day— diagnosis day—we told each other. We hugged and kissed the boys good-bye before pulling out of Patty's driveway. They would stay with their aunt for the three days we'd be gone. Terri smiled at her boys but didn't say much. By now she was stuttering and didn't want to struggle with a long speech for them to be good and not give their aunt Patty any trouble.

The drive to Jacksonville was long but without incident. Naturally, we made a couple of bathroom stops along the way. I wheeled her into the restroom each time with little thought as to how it looked to anyone. We had no choice in the matter. There were, of course, a few surprised glances at the sight of a man in a ladies' restroom, but most were compassionate and gave us the courtesy we needed in what was clearly a difficult situation.

We decided that we liked Jacksonville the second we pulled in. It looked like a huge city under strict manicure watch. The sense of order and calm were just what we needed. Once we checked into the hotel attached to the clinic, we made our way across the walkway to meet with our doctors.

The minute we set foot in the hospital we felt instantly better. Ready with a smile and a few light quips, the doctors and staff almost made us forget why we were there to begin with. They began with a cursory explanation about ALS and the mechanics of the brain's relationship with one's motor neuron cells. Then they went into the process of elimination they'd be taking us through in order to make an accurate diagnosis. Alzheimer's, Lyme disease …you name it; they were going to test for all of them. As they explained what the next couple of days would entail, they smiled and let us know that they were going to be nothing if not thorough. We felt the hope in us soar. The young Harvard-trained doctor ended by saying that if it indeed turned out to be ALS, then we would want to consider professional care and get Terri a breathing machine. I admit that I dismissed his warnings. I told myself that this was *not* going to be ALS. I told myself that the doctor was saying that only because he had to.

Having been through all the tests once before, we almost felt like veterans. Very little that was said was new to us. This time, however, I was given the task of collecting Terri's urine sample over the next twenty-four hours at certain intervals, starting that night. Tests would begin the following morning. We thanked them and made our way to the nearby grocery store to pick up some organic food to cook in the room's kitchenette. That night, as we began collecting her urine, Terri smiled and started to apologize for giving me so much work to do. I laughed.

"Terri, don't you see the upside to all of this?" I asked, as I reached for her underwear for the fifth time that evening.

"There's a plus to all of this?" she asked.

"Absolutely! I'm pretty sure I already qualify as a Guinness World Record contender for being the man who's pulled down the most panties in a twenty-four-hour period! And if that doesn't make me the envy of all men, I don't know what would!"

The following day, rested and eager to proceed, we made our way over to the clinic. Before long, we encountered the same villains we had met at the hospital in Homestead—the blood tests, PET scans, nerve conduction tests, and, yes, the foot-long spinal tap needle. This time I stayed in front of her, holding her hand and reassuring her that it would soon be over. She squeezed my hand the entire time, her eyes closed while she held her breath. I swore I never wanted to see her go through that again. I kissed her forehead when it was all over. All we had to do now was wait.

That night we had our first scare. We were in our room, relaxing and watching some mindless television. I was on the couch while Terri sat across from me in her wheelchair. With dinner and her bath already taken care of, we were enjoying a relaxing moment. It had been a long time since we'd been alone like this, with no kids to take care of and nothing to do.

Suddenly, and for no particular reason that I can identify, I sensed the need to look at her. That's when I saw her eyes flashing at mine, widening with fear as if in a silent scream. Sitting up, I frowned and asked her what was wrong. Unable to gesticulate with her arms or make a sound, she shot her eyes at the telephone beside me and repeated the motion a second time. It was then that I saw she was struggling to breathe. One second later I snapped out of my frozen state, grabbed the receiver, and dialed 911.

The few short minutes it took for the paramedics to arrive felt like the day that would never come. As soon as they pulled up, my stomach fell from my throat back to its rightful place as they ran to my wife's side. They began giving her oxygen while preparing her for the short ride to the hospital. I pulled back to give them room to work. But much to their disbelief, she still wasn't taking in air. They maintained their calm but commanding composures as they kept trying. Inside I was swimming in panic.

By now I had found my voice and began telling them about Terri's diagnosis. That's when they realized what was happening. Her diaphragm, the muscle that draws the air in, had stopped working. Now I could see the worry in their eyes as they kept trying. The panic in me surged. By now we were at the hospital. Then, through some precious miracle, Terri suddenly began taking air in and resumed breathing on her own.

We were shaken for the rest of the night. It hit me for the first time that this ALS—if it was indeed the culprit—could be every bit as horrible as we were being told. The doctor's warning about professional care and a breathing machine now rang in my ears. Is this where we were headed? Was this really happening? Was this our reality now?

The next day we met with the doctors. The tests, they said, concluded that while Terri was supremely healthy in every other way, she did, in fact, have "PLS," or primary lateral sclerosis. The degeneration of her upper body had begun; the lower would soon follow. Believe it or not, the news buoyed us with some hope. PLS was the *precursor* to ALS. She didn't have ALS. Not yet. We decided that we could—and would—find a way to stop the disease in its tracks before it went to the next level. We would not allow it to become ALS. The doctors did not let us leave without hearing their words of sympathy, and repeated warnings that we needed to consider getting professional help. They even went as far as to suggest a timeline. One year. She could be in need of a respirator within one year.

"Are you suggesting that I put her in a home?" I asked. And that, in essence, was what they were saying.

The hospital had a small but beautiful park with benches and shaded seating for patients and visitors to rest. When we left the hospital building, we found ourselves in that spot without knowing how we actually got there. We were in a complete daze.

All around us, family scenes of different kinds were being played out; there were smiles, laughter … tears, blank stares. Above us the sun was warm but not hot. We made our way to an area under a huge gumbo limbo tree, where it instantly felt a little cooler. When we came to a stop, I put my hand on Terri's head and stroked her hair gently. That's when she broke down and wept. I fell to my knees and wrapped my arms around her shoulders, my mouth close to her ear.

"Terri," I whispered as I swallowed my own tears. "Honey, I'll look after you," I said to my wife. "Don't think for a moment that I'm going to put you in a home. No way. *I'll* be your caregiver."

She shook in my arms and tried to speak. "Y … y … you … ca … can't—" she started to say.

I squeezed her even more tightly. "Yes! Yes, I can, honey. And I will. You'll see. We can beat this thing, Terri. I know we can!"

"Too … too much."

"Never mind what the doctor said. *I* will look after you. Do you hear me?"

"No … too much—"

"Terri, I am not about to toss you into a home where you'll be just another patient sitting in some corner waiting to see a familiar face. I'd have to move in with you if that were the case! No. I want you at home with everything and everyone you love around you every minute of the day. Besides, *I* need you at home. Don't you understand? The boys do too! We're a family now and always will be. ALS is not going to change any of that!"

"Robert—"

"No, honey! Listen to me. At home you'll still be a wife and a mother. Our family can't work without you. Don't you know that?"

The heaviness of the air inside the car—that's what I remember most from our visit to the Mayo Clinic. It hung there, draped around us like a cloak we couldn't pry off no matter what we did. To be honest, I'm not even sure how I was able to sit behind the wheel. While I focused on the impatient drivers trying to make it to their destination in half the time, my wife wept on and off, her eyes red and swollen. The helplessness I felt gripped me at my throat as I focused on breathing. I was your typical man when it came to wanting to fix things. If there was a problem before me, my knee-jerk reaction was to go solution hunting—even if it was a quick fix. Now all I could do was watch my wife cry the most painful tears I had ever seen. I never felt more desperate than I did in that car.

After an hour I just couldn't take it any longer. I wanted to find an escape for us both—an escape to a time and place that did not include tears, ALS—or any illness, for that matter. So I did the only thing I could do. I became an insensitive dolt and selected a CD by one of our favorite bands. The Fab 5 was a popular Jamaican band we had hired on a couple occasions to play at one of our many parties at our home. They were the kind of group that had everyone wanting to jump onto the dance floor. As the music started playing, I sang along, trying to smile and hoping to get Terri to do the same. Looking back, I still can't believe how stupid a move that was ... but I was that desperate. I wanted nothing more than to chase the monster away.

"Hey, honey," I said. "I have a great idea! How about we throw another party this Christmas, huh? We could invite all our friends and do a *huge* thing! Bigger than we've ever done before! It'll be fun!"

I glanced to my right actually hoping to see a happy reaction. But the look she shot me said it all.

"Y ... your ... f ... fault," she said. "T ... too much ... work! M ... made me s ... sick!"

"What ...?" Terri's words sliced into my heart. "But, Terri, how could—"

"Stress! All the stress!"

"You can't mean that, honey."

"Yes!"

"Terri, the doctors said—"

"Don't want to talk now!"

"Okay, honey. Okay."

Terri was blaming me for her ALS.

I turned the music off. I swallowed my hurt and stared ahead. In all our years of being married, I had never heard my wife say one hurtful word to me. Not one. I knew in my heart she didn't mean what she had just said. I knew it was the shock of the diagnosis, now confirmed. I got that she was frightened, confused, and devastated. I understood all that. And yet the sting of her words stayed with me like a rash on my skin.

For the rest of the way back to Miami, we drove in silence.

If I've learned anything from life, it's that, sometimes, the darkest times can bring us to the brightest places. I've learned that the most toxic people can teach us the most important lessons; that our most painful struggles can grant us the most necessary growth; and that the most heartbreaking losses of friendship and love can make room for the most wonderful people. I've learned that what seems like a curse in the moment can actually be a blessing, and that what seems like the end of the road is actually just the discovery that we are meant to travel down a different path. I've learned that no matter how difficult things seem, there is always hope. And I've learned that no matter how powerless we feel, or how horrible things seem, we can't give up. We have to keep going. Even when it's scary, even when all of our strength seems gone, we have to keep picking ourselves back up and moving forward, because whatever we're battling in the moment, it will pass, and we will make it through. We've made it this far. We can make it through whatever comes next.

—Daniell Keopke

CHAPTER 9

Sometimes You Need Darkness to See the Light

After the Mayo Clinic, we returned to our new normal in our little apartment. Still trying to relieve the sting of disbelief with frequent applications of hope, I went on the Internet and bought a few books on caregiving. I figured I needed to familiarize myself with the stages of emotions that a serious or terminal illness can put a family through. It was probably the most reading I'd ever done on a single subject. By not sugarcoating the situation we were in, the books did in fact help prepare me for what was to come. But more than anything, they told me the one thing I needed to hear—that we were not alone.

And so we waited for that first week in December when we would finally see the esteemed Dr. Bradley. Terri still held on to some level of independence by alternating between the walker and the wheelchair, which we had now upgraded to a motorized version. I continued to make my intermittent long weekend jaunts to Jamaica to try to either revive Wassi Art's sluggish sales or, better yet, find a buyer for our troubled enterprise.

I did my best to hide my quiet panic. With Editscope still not generating a profit by this point, cash flow was heavy on my mind. I was grateful that we even had an asset to sell, but I also knew there was a big difference between *wanting* to sell it as opposed to *having* to. The truth was that life now felt as if it were on a seesaw that had suddenly found itself stuck in one direction—pointing downward. If we were to get Terri cured, we'd need money. We had medical insurance, but there was only so much it could do. And we had the boys to look after too. So I continued to take my short trips in an effort to make *something* happen, always arranging for Patty or some other family member to check in on Terri. I didn't want her to be alone longer than was necessary. I hated being away but felt I had no choice.

One morning, the inevitable happened. With the boys at school, Terri had been trying to move around with her walker, taking her time as she had grown accustomed to doing. She had managed to make herself a light breakfast and change out of her nightclothes. But once she got to the small bathroom, she lost her balance and slipped. She fell to the floor in between the toilet and the sink, her head narrowly missing the porcelain bowl. Unable to move and shaking from the fall, she kept full-blown panic at bay by telling herself that sooner or later Patty would call to check on her. She would call. A couple hours later, the phone rang. Terri would tell me afterward that she had never been so happy to hear the sweet shrill of the telephone. When Terri didn't answer, Patty got into her car and drove over to see what had happened to her sister.

I felt the weight of pure guilt slam against me when I finally heard what had happened. I decided that from then on, if I ever had to travel, no matter how short the trip, Terri would have to come with me. I didn't care how much extra work it would be with her having to travel on wheels. It was not an inconvenience, I told her, just a matter of doing things differently. She tried to assure me that it wasn't necessary, but I wouldn't hear it. I made good on my promise, and my wife accompanied me from then on. It was on one of those trips, in the middle of the short flight down to Montego Bay, that I had the chance to show her that ALS wasn't going to scare us that easily. About forty-five minutes into the flight, Terri signaled that she needed to relieve herself.

With the bathroom in the airplane as small as it is, we always tried to ensure that she had the chance to empty her bladder just minutes before boarding the aircraft. On that particular flight, however, a delay on the tarmac before takeoff had extended the time beyond her ability to hold it.

"I'm sorry, honey," she said with a grimace as she whispered into my ear. "I don't think I can hold it until we land. What are we going to do?"

"What are we going to do?" I smiled at her. "*This* is what we're going to do."

I stood up, bent down, scooped her off her seat with both arms, and carried her down the aisle to the bathroom. I didn't even have to signal to the flight attendant closest to us. She met us at the bathroom and held the door open for us. She turned to face away from us. I stood with my back to the door so as to give Terri privacy and allow her some dignity. She was a good sport about it and smiled with a wink.

On returning to our seats, we were met by a sudden applause and cheering by the other passengers. We smiled back and even laughed a little with some mild embarrassment. Terri beamed like a young bride as some of the ladies congratulated her on having a good man for a husband.

"It's one like that I want," one lady shouted.

"Girl, you'd better hold on to that man," said another.

"I bet you wouldn't do that for me," accused another of her husband sitting quietly next to her.

"Now, that's what I'm talking about!" said still another.

91

I admit to turning a couple shades of red but enjoying the moment. It lifted our spirits. In some respects, it even helped make us feel like any other couple.

December finally arrived. We held our breaths as we mentally and emotionally prepared ourselves for the meeting on which our final hopes were hinged. Located at the University of Miami, Dr. Bradley's office was a short drive away. It would mimic our time with him. A senior doctor with decades of experience, he didn't take long to assess the tests that had already been done by both hospitals. With a businesslike demeanor, he confirmed his agreement with the conclusions. It was ALS.

Any hope we had left at that point now had to be checked at the door. We sat there, somewhat prepared, and yet still feeling that God, life, and the universe had all let us down. How we kept breathing, I can't say. How we didn't melt out of our skins and sink into the floor and call it quits then and there, I don't know. I can only tell you that all around us, outside in the lobby, around the hospital, outside on the streets, life continued moving forward with no acknowledgment that we had just been dealt the biggest blow of our lives.

With as much compassion as he could muster, Dr. Bradley repeated the suggestion made by the doctors at the Mayo Clinic that we make plans to seek professional care. He looked straight at us. This disease, he said, was a particularly dreadful one. While we could not possibly understand the extent of it, we should nevertheless heed his plea to take it seriously. ALS had a mind of its own and could progress rapidly overnight. Not only would Terri need 'round-the-clock care, she would eventually need a machine to help her breathe.

As if sensing that we still hadn't fully accepted what we were faced with, he made it clear that nothing we had ever gone through before in life could possibly have prepared us for what was yet to come. And come it would, he assured us. The disease would run its course. If real help was not secured, it could take its toll on the caregiver. As for Terri, he said the most he could do was prescribe her Rilutek to help slow down the onset of some of the symptoms. But there were side effects too, he warned, side effects serious enough to require testing of her liver every month, without fail.

We took the prescription, shook hands with the doctor, thanked him, and left. The consultation with Bradley would mark the very last time we met with any conventional doctor concerning Terri's ALS.

This time on the drive back, there were no tears. We kept the radio low as we allowed our thoughts to roam. Terri kept her gaze forward, barely looking at me. Apart from her insisting that she was not going to take the drugs prescribed, we agreed that she was to continue with physical therapy treatment and her massages with Patty. After that we said very little. At first I thought that we were taking the news better this time around after having heard it twice before. But, in hindsight, I believe that on that day, Terri began to slip into a darkness that she had not allowed herself to enter before now.

I couldn't blame her. I had thought her amazingly strong for not falling into depression sooner. She had a life spirit enough for ten lifetimes, no question about it. But even the strong grow tired and need to rest their weary limbs and spirits, if even for a short while. This was new territory for me. Never before had I seen my Terri in this … this place. There was no manual to consult. No one to offer advice. I kept my eyes looking forward, still telling myself that we would find a way out of this sick darkness.

In the days immediately following our consultation with Dr. Bradley, Terri turned inward. Suddenly she grew quiet, not always reacting to my attempts to share a joke or entertain her with idle chatter. The smiles were fewer now. Treats that would normally have produced a nod instead resulted in a slow shaking of the head. Whenever I attempted to touch her hand or stroke her hair, she responded in an almost robotic way. It was as if the life had already flown out of her soul. Her eyes looked like they'd turned the lights out forever. I now began to hear her weep in private. Sometimes she'd stop when I came into the room. Other times she'd look away as if not wanting to trust me with her sorrow. For the first time in my life I had no answers, no solutions, no quick fixes. I was mentally and emotionally paralyzed in a way that I'd never been in all my days of living. I'll be honest—it felt like she'd already left us.

The boys sensed her withdrawal too. Alex in particular retreated even further into his own world. He had begun to almost completely refuse to go to her. The resentment and anger on his part were obvious enough. Why he felt this way, however, I couldn't say. Perhaps he felt burdened by having a sick parent to worry about. Maybe he was resentful of the fact that our entire family dynamics had been altered because of her. Or maybe he felt a sense of abandonment. Perhaps it was just plain fear. I knew it was a problem that needed to be addressed, but I admit that I was neither able nor in the mood to broach the topic with my son. To be frank, I just didn't have the energy.

Justin—always a little more demonstrative in his love for his mother—hovered instinctively close by to help if she needed him. But even he knew to keep a safe distance so as to not be hurt by her mood swings.

After a few days, Terri took to the Internet once again. Whether she was looking for quiet companionship or a cure, or both, I didn't know at the time. She was sharing very little with us now. We had no choice but to watch and wait.

Meanwhile, she continued her diet of organic foods with an emphasis on meats. But soon she began to talk about feeling uncomfortable. Her bowel movements, she mentioned, were starting to feel less normal. I sensed a change coming but decided to wait for her signal.

As the daylight hours grew shorter in the winter months, my days began to feel darker and heavier. It wasn't long before I found myself not responding as quickly as I used to in the beginning whenever Terri needed something. With personal exercise time already a thing of the past, I was no longer feeling as nimble or energetic as I used to. But if I were being completely honest, I'd say that it probably had more to do with common complacency. I think it's a natural mechanism of one's brain to "forget" as a way of emotional survival. I suppose if we lived every waking moment with the fear of our situation at the fore, we'd shut down and remain paralyzed. But, try as I did to remind myself every waking second that she was going through a personal hell, I found that I was not always able to stay in that zone of continuous empathy. The pull of *my* "normal" was still stronger at this point.

For example, if I was in the middle of watching a favorite television show and she signaled that she needed something, I would sometimes ask her if it could wait until a bit later, depending on what it was. I admit that once or twice I caught myself frowning with mild irritation for having been interrupted by her. On those occasions, she would merely look at me and go deeply silent, the frustration etched in her face.

Was I being lazy? Possibly.

Insensitive? Perhaps.

Did I feel a little guilty about it? Of course.

Other times she'd snap at me when she felt I hadn't done something quite right or fast enough, her eyes going dark or unable to look at me for too long. And then one day, after another low-keyed outburst, she finally said it.

"Why don't you just put me in a home and forget about me?" The anger cut through me like a newly sharpened knife. I snapped back in a knee-jerk reaction to echo her attack.

"Look, Terri, if that's what you want, then fine." To this day, it is this sentence I regret uttering the most. If I could take anything back in this life, it is that heated reply. But then you can't "unring" a bell, can you? Once you say something you regret, the most you can hope for is that the person forgives you … because it's unlikely he or she will ever quite be able to forget. The fact is, words have the power to hurt or heal.

In all our married life, this was the most tension we'd ever had between us. Underneath it all, I secretly wondered how she could still blame her former busy life—and therefore *me*—for causing her ALS. Despite the fact that all three doctors had insisted that the cause of ALS was yet unknown, why did she insist on laying blame at my feet? I had given her a wonderful life, I reasoned with myself … given her everything she could ever want. Now she was blaming the very person who had made it all possible.

My own research on the role of the caregiver helped me somewhat at this juncture. I knew to expect this phase of anger and resentment. I understood intellectually that in the case of terminal illness, or a dramatically changed life due to other events such as a stroke or an accident, that the closest caregiver and family members would bear the brunt of the blame and anger. But expecting the flames to erupt and understanding the dynamics behind it didn't exactly make it easier to take once it actually scorched your skin. No matter how you explained it away, it still hurt. It still burned.

I ran the questions through my mind.

Haven't I been doing everything she asks?

Am I not taking care of her myself as I promised, instead of shutting her away in a home as everyone said I should?

Am I not enabling her to maintain some dignity as a wife and mother by being her sole caregiver?

And am I not still showing her the love of a devoted husband?

As hard as it is to admit, even now that she's gone, my own resentment started to stir. It lingered and gained traction in my heart. It didn't help that some of the few friends and family who by now knew about her illness were already encouraging me to get professional help. Or, worse, put her in a home. I began to wonder if they were right. Was I crazy for thinking I could do this on my own?

"You can't continue doing this, Robert."

"You're going to end up driving yourself into the ground."

"She'll have to understand that one person simply cannot do this. It's not humanly possible."

"You're crazy, man."

The comments kept coming. Sometimes they came directly. Sometimes, not. A couple of them stung:

"She's being too demanding."

"She doesn't appreciate what you're doing for her."

The tension that had wormed its way between us lingered like a wintery chill that wouldn't leave. I did my best to ignore it. Time, I said. We just needed time to return to "us" again. Still committed to tackling her ALS in a holistic way, I decided to incorporate even more massage therapy into her weekly treatment. With Patty's help, we found a massage therapist with a studio not far from the office. It would work out perfectly, I thought. I'd take her there a couple times a week after lunch, and time it so that once the session was over, we'd go pick up the boys from school.

Terri began her sessions with her new therapist. But within a few weeks, I began to sense a shift in her. It began with her asking me to massage her in the way that he did. To be honest, I thought nothing of it and, in fact, assumed it meant that the sessions were helping her. I had never had any training, of course, but I listened to her instructions and did my best.

Then one morning while we were getting her dressed for our trek to the office, she asked me to select a particular outfit from her closet. The clothing she wanted that day was not her usual choice of loose-fitting track pants and blouse. Today she chose something decidedly more sophisticated. More attractive. I also noticed that she had somehow managed to apply some light makeup. She was normally one to use makeup only for special occasions, and I thought that perhaps she was trying to boost her spirits while the in grip of a dark phase.

Later that day, however, when we got to the lobby and headed toward the elevator, she stopped and told me that I didn't have to take her up to the studio; she could take it from here. I remember feeling surprised, but I said nothing. If holding on to some level of independence made her feel better about herself, I told myself, then I was all for it. I heard myself saying this, and yet something didn't feel quite right. Over the next couple of weeks, the trend continued. Terri paid close attention to her attire on her massage days, and she insisted on going up the elevator herself. Now the questions inside me began to beat faster.

One night, after the children had gone to sleep, we were in our room. The evening news was on the television. I had already given Terri her bath and tucked her into bed, the sheets and blanket pulled up to cover her chest. I sat in a chair next to the bed instead of sitting up in the bed as I usually did. I tried to concentrate on the television screen, but my mind kept wandering to the growing knot in my stomach. Part of me did not want to ask her that certain question, the answer to which I wasn't sure I was prepared to hear. Eventually, with my mouth already dry and my heart pounding, I reached for the remote control and lowered the volume. She turned to look at me.

"Terri," I began, taking a deep breath and looking at the floor. "I need to ask you a question." There was no smile on my face or in my tone. Both were flat. She frowned.

"Something wrong?" Her speech had by now deteriorated to the point where she sounded as if she were speaking with marbles in her mouth. She had also gotten into the habit of shortening her sentences to make up for the extra time it took to make herself understood.

I raised my eyes and looked straight at her. "That's what I was wondering. Is there something wrong? With us, I mean."

She looked at me straight, not blinking or moving her head. "Don't understand."

I took another deep breath. "It's just that I've noticed a change in you ever since you started going to this ... this masseur. I mean, all of a sudden you're dressing different. Now you no longer want me to take you up to the studio." I paused to see if she wanted to stop me, but she said nothing. "I ... I'm sorry, but I just don't have a good feeling about it. I have to ask. I have to know because it's keeping me up at night. Look, there has never been a single secret between us. So I'm asking. Is there something going on with this guy that I should know about?"

Terri shut her eyes and swallowed hard. She shook her head and began to shake. The tears came a second later. "No."

"Nothing's happened with him?"

"No."

"But then why are you crying?" I remained where I sat, wanting to go to her but unsure about what she would say next. She cried for a few seconds more before taking a deep breath.

"Was angry. So angry. ALS. Make me ugly. Ugly woman."

"But, Terri, I've told you so many times that—"

"No. Need to finish. Want to tell you. Know it is hard to take care of me. Sick wife. Every day. Every night. Every minute. Like baby. Know you must be tired. You do things most cannot. Most won't. Maybe you get tired soon. Or angry too. No longer love me. He … made me feel pretty again. Like real woman. Think … maybe last chance to feel attractive. Before get worse. Before you leave me. Leave this sick wife you didn't ask for. Know that someday soon you leave this wife with stiff, frozen body. Leave me for normal woman. Healthy woman."

My stomach fell out from under me. I watched my wife's face collapse into agony. Through deep gasps and a stream of tears, she apologized for allowing herself to feel that way, and for acting on her deepest fears and taking what had amounted to a preemptive strike. I had been so good to her, she said. She knew I loved her, but she worried that over time I'd begin to love her less as the disease took over and eventually changed her into a piece of unwanted furniture. She repeated that she loved me and that she was raging at God and the universe for giving her a disease she didn't deserve. "I live life of good person," she said. "Do no harm. Help people. Love God. Love family, friends. Why me? Why ALS?" It would be the only time in her twelve-year battle with the disease that I'd ever hear her express words of self-pity.

In the end, she admitted to having fallen into a deep depression since our consultation with Dr. Bradley. When she finally stopped speaking, she looked at me with eyes that said more than words could.

I didn't move. Instead, I gathered all my strength to keep the hurt and anger I felt at a safe distance. I had moved heaven and earth to make her comfortable. Was that not enough? I closed my eyes and said nothing for a while, trying instead to put myself in her position. If I were the one staring my death sentence in the face, what would I do? How would I be thinking? Where would my mind turn to? How lost and frightened would I be?

I won't hesitate to admit that in the days and weeks that followed, I retreated into my own depression. Dark circles began to appear under my eyes as I went about my days in a semi-robotic state. The betrayal, the hurt, the anger … they all sat there like mystery doors waiting for me to choose one and cross the threshold. Instead, I remained frozen. I was numb. I didn't know what to feel. Worse, I didn't know what to do.

For the brief time that Terri remained in her angry period, I came close to losing faith in my promise to her. I admit now that I began feeling sorry for myself and thought seriously about giving up. *Maybe I really should find a home for her,* I thought. *Just walk away. Find a new life for me. Do what most would have done. At least I could say I tried.*

It wasn't that I felt she was being demanding. The way I saw it, if love was the motivation behind anything you did, then nothing asked of you could be considered a chore or a burden. And I loved her. Terri could have asked me to do anything. Anything. I'd have done it with a full heart.

What I was beginning to doubt, however, was my ability to make her smile again. Could I still make her happy as her husband? Was our marriage, and our family, going to survive this disease? Did she love me as she used to? Did that even matter now? Was she focused only on her inevitable passing? And if so, wasn't that to be expected under the circumstances? Could I not forgive her for thinking desperate—even out-of-character—thoughts at a time like this? Was I perhaps being selfish for even focusing on my hurt feelings, as I was now? I asked the question of myself again. What would *my* state of mind be if I thought I might be dying? Would anything but my own comfort and desires matter if I knew that my days were numbered? If I were being truly honest with myself, would I not have done or considered worse?

I reflected on the events that had come my way in the recent past, and I started to connect the dots. At this point, I needed something to make sense. My brother's death ... the retreat with the Missionaries of the Poor ... even the beggar in the summer storm. Were all those part of some plan that God or the universe, or both, had in store for me? Were they stepping-stones laid before me in preparation for an even greater challenge? And was my wife's illness the test I was destined to face all along?

Sometimes while alone, I felt the fear creeping into my skin as I questioned the future, what was yet to come, and my ability to survive it. My hands often went damp as I closed my eyes and took in deep, deliberate breaths. At times I'd pray but not with constructed sentences ... it was more like willing my soul to be infused with the wisdom of the universe. Because I needed that more than ever—the wisdom and the strength to get through this.

And then one day I just stopped. *Live in the moment, Robert,* I reminded myself. *Isn't that what you've always done? Don't be afraid of what you can't understand. The future will come regardless of how hard you try to see it in advance. Stop wasting your energy fighting it. Don't cloud your head with fear, or you'll never find a way to steady your mind and feet so you can move forward. Whatever the incident is, whatever the bad news may be, whatever the situation that makes you want to pivot and run, just accept it for what it is. It's a life lesson. It's a challenge you have to face. You know what to do,* I told myself. *You've done it before. Simply accept the situation and move forward.*

My own period of introspection was brief. When it was over, I wiped away my tears of frustration. If there was one thing I knew without a doubt, it was that I loved my wife and my family. Mistakes happen. Emotions get in the way. But I also knew that love was only a word if it didn't include constant acts of kindness. And hadn't we promised to be kind to one another when we married?

In the end I forgave her. I decided that it was the insanity of having to stare mortality in the face that had caused my beloved wife—this brave woman—to lose her balance. It was not a position that I could fully appreciate or understand, and I reminded myself that I needed to be thankful for that. I told myself that I owed her my compassion. She was, after all, a human being fighting the most basic challenge of all—to stay alive.

I have no doubt that many will dismiss me as just a man who was, to put it politely, besotted by his wife. But I know bravado for what it is—nothing more than an insecure man's crutch. In the end I blessed the problem and embraced the opportunity to turn things around.

Compassion begins at home, and it is not how much we do but how much love we put into that action. Do not think that love has to be extraordinary. What we need is to love without getting tired.

—Mother Theresa

CHAPTER 10

Trump Tragedy with Triumph

By the time 2003 arrived, I had concocted a two-pronged plan. I would find a way to get more exercise into Terri's life, and maybe even get her walking again to some degree. And I would do everything I could to make her feel like any other woman—not a wife or mother, but a woman, period. I'd woo her out of her dark state and back into my arms, just like a courting lover. I needed her to understand that she still had the ability to arouse me, despite the wheelchair, despite the frustrations of her slurred speech, and even despite the fact that she could do less for herself now than could a small child. To me, none of it really mattered.

As strange as it may sound, I paid almost no attention to the fact that so much about her physical aspect had changed. My mind, my memories, my feelings—they had all converged like a funnel, allowing me to see her only as the energetic, life-loving, beautiful woman who had made my heart soar the first time we met. I didn't see her as an invalid or a patient to be pitied. I wasn't turned off—as I'm sure many around us wondered about. No. I still felt for my wife the way I did the first time I touched her at the Dover racetrack. I didn't even have to try to convince myself. It was all there, unaltered and unaffected. True love—*real love*—transcends sexual attraction.

The moments I capitalized on most were the ones that came after I had bathed her and washed her hair. Using light touches, I'd towel-dry her slowly, not holding back the smile in my eyes, not trying to hurry the process so I could get it over with, not thinking about whatever it was that I could be doing instead of taking care of her. I'd do the same when combing her hair or applying lotion to her entire body. Soft, easy strokes, like a gentle massage that wouldn't end when the hour was up. Inevitably the experience would prove itself to me ... and to her ... to be pleasurable. And that's when I'd turn to her and say until I no longer had to: "Look at what you're doing to me!" And just for emphasis, I'd glance downward. ALS did not destroy our sex life. We continued to be fairly active, in fact. Naturally I had to do all the work, but that didn't bother me. I learned very quickly about being creative. I continued to pleasure my wife in the way that I had always done before. From this point on, not once did it ever occur to us that we should cease enjoying one another.

The exercise routine I came up with was based on a very simple, if not naïve, theory. If her brain was no longer sending signals to her muscles, then perhaps we could remind her muscles how to work independent of those signals. Yes, that's right. After three separate confirmations by highly qualified doctors, I *still* thought we could beat ALS. And so I came up with the plan of tying one of my leather belts around her waist, keeping it snug. I'd hold the belt behind her and follow her as she took one step at a time. If she could still walk with the walker, then all she needed to do was work on her balance. That was my big groundbreaking theory. Neither of us believed our efforts to be futile. We never once questioned it. In fact, we practiced our little belt exercise routine several times a day.

It's frightening enough to be sick, even while under a doctor's care. Essentially on our own with no doctor to guide us, I went in search of assistance of a different kind. I didn't know what to look for exactly, but I started googling anyway. Eventually I came across something called Pilates therapy. This was completely new to me, so I made sure to spend some time looking under the hood before sharing the information with Terri. After some reading, I decided that it sounded promising. Brent Anderson was the name that kept coming up as one of the leading names in the modern-day industry. With a PhD in physical therapy, he was also an orthopedic certified specialist who lectured in Miami and worldwide. I searched for his image and saw an individual with kindness in his eyes. That was important to me. I wanted nothing but warmth for Terri. If you were going to come into contact with her, you needed to come into her space with love.

Originally based in California, where he had had his first facility, Dr. Anderson had recently relocated to Miami in 1997 in the Coral Gables area. He was not thirty minutes from where we lived. I decided to take that as a sign we were meant to seek his help. I immediately booked Terri's regular sessions with him.

Meanwhile, she began to mention that she wasn't having the usual sensation of needing to go to the bathroom to empty her bowels. It was particularly frustrating, as she had already lost some amount of bladder control. At first she tried wearing adult protection to prevent accidents while out in public, but she hated it. I told her to abandon them altogether and to just let me know whenever she needed to go. Now we turned to the matter of her bowel movements.

"This just gets increasingly romantic, doesn't it?" she quipped with a sigh. "I know I need to go. I'm clearly distended from all the food I've been eating. But I'm not having that urge."

We checked with her brother, who agreed that she seemed to have lost peristalsis movement in her colon. He confirmed, however, that that was not usually associated with ALS. We made arrangements to have her colon tested for blockages. Meanwhile, I began giving her enemas to help clear her. I decided the best thing to do was to lay her down on a towel in the bathroom so that the commute to the toilet was as short as could be. She grimaced apologetically when I made my first attempt.

"First you have to clean me up like a baby—number ones and number twos. And now … now you have to give me enemas." She closed her eyes as if not wanting to see my face. "I guess you didn't exactly have this in mind when you vowed 'for better or for worse.'"

The frustration in her voice nicked me like a paper cut. I understood that this was not Terri the wife talking, but Terri the woman who had once known what it was like to feel whole, functional, independent, beautiful … sensuous. She knew I still adored her. But was that self-confidence now being eroded by waves of embarrassment and shame? Was she now seeing herself as a woman without dignity? Did she still think I no longer desired her even after my many attempts to convince her otherwise?

I decided not to ask questions. Instead, I focused on action. After successfully administering the enema, I gently caressed her bare behind with my hand and told her that I had to be the luckiest man in the world for having such a sexy enema patient.

She gave me a small smile of appreciation and then congratulated me on a job well done. "I didn't know you had so many hidden talents."

"Maybe it's not too late for me to get my nursing degree," I joked. "But I'd want you to be my only patient!" Maybe it wasn't my best joke. I was nervous and knew that it was a poor attempt at grief-masking. Terri wasn't easily fooled either. She knew I was still trying to find that happy place. The thing is, I had no more tricks up my sleeve. All I wanted to do was make her laugh. If I could just do that, then I knew we'd be okay.

She surprised me with a small joke of her own. "And there I was thinking I could pimp you out for a small fee." I could sense the effort behind her attempt and was encouraged. We were both trying.

"Sorry, I'm not available. Please tell your customers that I'm already booked solid by one very special woman!"

My wife smiled again. But this time it felt more instinctive. There was almost a sigh of relief behind it. It was all I needed.

I continued to flirt with Terri at every opportunity. I was going to make her feel like a woman again in every sense of the word, no matter how long it took me. One way or another, I would convince her.

Meanwhile, as we waited for her appointment at the hospital to check her colon, Terri went on instinct and returned to her holistic doctor as part of her recovery and wellness army.

The day before her colon test, Terri followed the hospital's orders and drank copious amounts of an oil-based substance to clear her bowels. She barely held it down. The barium test itself the following day was not any easier. She just managed to keep it in her stomach, although I swore that if she even breathed too deeply, it was going to come flying out. Then, as if to challenge her further, the hospital ended up testing the wrong part of the intestine, requiring her to repeat the whole procedure. But in the end we got good news. There were no blockages or tumors in her colon or intestines.

Her holistic doctor suggested again that she try hydrocolonic therapy.

"What's that?" I asked.

"Basically, it's the process of pushing water through your colon to clean it out," she explained. "Western medicine doesn't love the idea. In fact, they consider it harmful to the colon. But the more I read, the more sense it makes to me. So I want to go ahead with it."

She booked ten sessions with the doctor, who used an electrical machine for the procedure. She endured everything from discomfort to outright pain. The doctor suggested the culprit for the discomfort was a mass of gas in the intestines. After the sessions were over, however, she was no better than before she had walked into his office. She announced shortly after that she was switching to a vegan diet, and maybe even to a raw vegan diet.

"Vegan? Raw food?" I said, sounding like a ten-year-old suddenly discovering that he was going to be eating peas and carrots for dinner for the rest of his life. We were on our way to the office and had just pulled out of the driveway. "Vegan I get. But why raw? Isn't that a bit drastic?"

She nodded with a wry smile. "Well, I've been doing a lot of research," she said in an attempt to reassure me. "The cooking process actually destroys the enzymes that your body needs for real nourishment. So even though you're eating something that's good for you, once you add heat, you essentially change it. Then suddenly it's just not as helpful to your body. The benefits are reduced. I know it sounds extreme, honey, and you and the boys certainly don't have to follow along if you don't want to. I know it won't be easy. But after reading up on it, I know this can help me. And I don't have anything to lose. So here's my plan."

I turned the radio off so I could listen as Terri took her time to explain what she'd been reading for the past few weeks. By now her speech sounded as if it were on slow mode and based on mostly vowels. But I could understand her faster than anyone could. She seemed the least frustrated when speaking with me.

She had read that not only does the body have the ability to heal itself if given the right conditions, it can actually renew itself every seven years. And nourishing the body with foods in their purest state was the way to achieve this miracle.

"It's not a far-fetched theory. There are those who feel that the body can regenerate itself if a certain diet and way of life are followed. So if I can renew my body, why not my motor neurons too?"

I will admit that I wasn't as convinced. I was not the well-read person that my wife was. All I knew was that her eyes danced when she shared the information with me. She still had hope, and that was all I needed to know. We were already encouraged by the fact that the breathing incident that had happened at the Mayo Clinic had not repeated itself. It was a significant yardstick by which to measure her efforts. Terri felt sure that the changes she had made in her diet until then had something to do with it.

"So in theory it would be like having a new body," she continued. "And if my body can be reborn, then maybe it'll come back without ALS." I hugged her and said it sounded great. Her plan was a three-part treatment:

One. Stop putting new toxins in your body.

Two. Eliminate the toxins already in it.

Three. Rejuvenate and nourish.

We immediately embarked on stage one.

Terri ate nothing that required cooking, nor touched anything that had been processed to any degree. We got the best of anything organic that could be consumed in a raw form. Smoothies became her new favorite dish. But we didn't stop at just food. At her request, we went further and changed all the lightbulbs in the house from incandescent to radiation-free natural daylight bulbs. We threw out all chlorine-based cleaning products; installed filters to remove chlorine from the water, including in the shower; changed her personal hygiene toiletries to aluminum-free products; and asked that there be no smoking around her if we were with friends.

The list of changes grew as time passed. At times I struggled. This new way of living just seemed to be so ... well ... overwhelming. But I reminded myself that if I thought this was inconvenient, then imagine what life in a wheelchair must be like. She'd sometimes see the frustration in my face too and smile at me patiently. I think she understood that I was committed to getting her well again. But she also knew that I had to buff up my will every now and then. I guess sometimes I lost my own footing. All along, Terri exhibited extreme mind control. I took her cue. She led, and I followed like her personal recruit. Looking back, I realize she had enrolled me in a course in structure without my knowing it. And I probably needed it.

We continued her Pilates therapy sessions with Brent Anderson. She enjoyed his high energy and never missed an appointment. He, in turn, was so impressed with her incredibly positive attitude and our devotion to one another, that he asked us both to be his "show and tell" for one of his lectures at the University of Miami. We were only too happy to oblige him.

Some months later in the summer, we returned to Jamaica for a longer break and to check on Wassi Art. "As the universe would have it," Terri would later tell a friend, we just happened to discover a home-based hydrocolonic husband-and-wife therapist team not far from where we were staying. Initially wary after the first experience with her holistic doctor, Terri agreed to give it another shot. This new therapist assured her that his gravity-fed technique would prove more gentle and effective.

"Have faith, Terri. I can help you," was all he needed to say. He was a calm and poised, but jolly, individual with the kind of natural warmth you're only too happy to sink into. Within seconds of meeting us he had us in stitches, making us almost forget the reason we'd come for his help. His personality was in sharp contrast with the nature of the service he was providing. We relaxed, and she agreed to try it one more time.

"Well, what else do I have on my hot agenda?" she quipped later when I asked her if she was sure about trying this again. The truth was that I was afraid she'd face disappointment once more. "I never thought I'd be so obsessed with such basic matters as bowel movements. But now that I've lost that going feeling, I want it back. I can't continue with the enemas, Robert. I've got to fix this."

The therapist delivered on his promise. Taking a more comprehensive approach, he treated Terri with reflexology using a high-force machine before each hydrocolonic session, gave her coffee enemas to cleanse the liver, and used an herb called cat's claw to heal the intestines. He also had her detoxify once a week with a foot ionic machine, which involved her placing her bare feet in a small tub of warm water and salt. A weak electrical current was then transmitted in order to encourage the toxins to start flowing out. The result was a gradual oozing of a ghastly gooey, yellow substance that came out of the bottom of her feet. It was, to be quite frank, disgusting.

Meanwhile, Terri took advantage of the fact that the sea was close by. Having been told that seawater was a natural form of detoxification, I made sure to take her to our special beach every day so she could feel the sun on her skin. It had a name, but we called it "Bubbles" because of the freshwater spring that lay beneath. When underwater, you could actually hear the sound of the springwater bubbling to the surface. It was our very own aquarium, a private sanctuary I'd often go to whenever I needed to shut the world out for a few minutes. But Terri was now sensitive to being even mildly cool. So we set a chair just below the point where the water broke onto the sand, and let her sit in the late afternoon sun so that the water could swirl around her legs and the sun could bathe her skin with its warmth and natural healing goodness.

She had also learned that ginger has powerful properties and is considered a healing spice in many parts of the Old World. Jamaican ginger has long been known for being particularly potent thanks to the rich minerals in the area's soil. So she drank several cups of tea made from it daily and had warm washcloths soaked in ginger water placed on her body where it felt the most stiff. I joined her for many cups of tea.

I asked her one night, as I was tucking her into bed, if she felt any improvement. That was our obsession—if not to make her well, then to make her better.

"Yes, some," she said with a smile. "I don't feel quite as rigid or stiff. Mind you, it doesn't last very long. But I'll take it!"

For the remainder of our time there, Terri continued with the ginger regimen, including it in her smoothies, fruit meals, and all her teas. Not long after we returned to Miami, she finally regained the peristalsis in her colon. She was functioning again with some level of dignity.

That relatively small victory alone almost had Terri leaping out of her wheelchair and walking again. Meanwhile, the sand in her hourglass continued to fall.

From One of Terri's Closest Friends:

My "little sister." That's what I used to call Terri. We were each other's confidante before and during her battle with ALS.

When she was first diagnosed, under the calm veneer existed anger and resentment. She was extremely bright—a lateral thinker and the nuts and bolts of the family unit who had spent a life working long hours and sorting things out. Robert was the visionary, but she made it happen. They truly made for the perfect couple. So to have to sit there, strapped to a wheelchair because she had become a rag doll, trapped in her body without the ability to even stretch her arms out to hug her boys and make everything all right for them and her husband ... well, the frustration was beyond palpable. But, as time passed, her anger evolved into an acceptance that if this was what God wanted, then she was going to live the best way she could. She was never the kind to give up hope, you see. Not Terri. Eventually she dabbled in New Age spirituality, a lot of which I didn't understand. But I suppose when your life is threatened, you look for the miracle everywhere and anywhere. When she went on the raw vegan diet, she was so transformed, her skin becoming so flawless, I began calling her my "little butterfly."

In the beginning she feared that Robert would not be there for her. Would he be able to do it? Would he stay with her? But after a while, when he proved otherwise, she grew confident and relaxed in his love. It says a lot about him that he stood up and faced his responsibilities as he did. I will never forget how he treated her broken body with such tenderness and respect. I know of few who would do what he did.

Whenever Terri came to Jamaica, I'd spend as much time as I could with her, holding her hand and talking with her. And when I say "talk," I mean we'd have a conversation in almost the true sense of the word, even when toward the end she could barely speak. I'd look at her and just know what she was thinking. I'd say a word, she'd confirm by nodding when she still could, and then blinking when she couldn't, and I'd finish the paragraph. I'd always feel as if I was in a holy place when with her. I always felt as if I had gained something for having sat with her.

Distance made no difference to our instinctive connection. On a few occasions, I got this feeling that something had gone wrong, and I called Robert only to find out that something had indeed gone terribly wrong. I remember two times in particular—the first was when they were at the Mayo Clinic in Jacksonville and she had had trouble breathing. I called just as the paramedics were working on her. The second happened when she'd fallen off the massage table. Again, I had this sudden feeling I wanted to speak with them, and I called just as they were taking her to the hospital. The blood was still fresh on her face from the fall.

I owe my life to Terri and Robert. I had my own health issues while she was battling ALS. Toward the end of her illness, I needed and had heart surgery, which failed. My doctors told me I'd need a second, but that I would have to heal from the first. So essentially I was dying while waiting. That's when Terri ordered Robert to send me an herbal supplement to help heal me and keep me alive so that I could have that second surgery. And he did … sent them by FedEx right away. I took them, healed, and lived long enough to go back to the surgeon's table. I'm here today because of them. I'm here because of my little butterfly.

—Cynthia Silvera

Breathe. It's okay. You're going to be okay. Just breathe. Breathe, and remind yourself of all the times in the past you've felt this scared. All of the times you felt this anxious and this overwhelmed. All of the times you felt this level of pain. And remind yourself how each time, you made it through. Life has thrown so much at you, and despite how difficult things have been, you've survived. Breathe and trust that you can survive this too. Trust that as long as you don't give up and keep pushing forward, no matter how hopeless things seem, you will make it.

—Daniell Koepke

CHAPTER 11

Have Faith No Matter What Form It Takes

Back in Miami, attending Mass at St. John Neumann Catholic Church continued to be our Sunday family ritual. I can honestly say that at first we genuinely enjoyed attending. The hour or two amid prayers and song with fellow believers calmed us. It made us focus our thoughts and energy and did its part to keep us together as a close-knit family. It was an extension of our life before we came to Miami that gave us a sense of continuity.

But for some time now, I could tell that our enthusiasm had begun to wane. At first we didn't voice it, probably because we didn't quite know what that growing emptiness was about. We had always believed in a higher being—had always held firm to the belief that prayers would eventually be answered if you kept at it long enough. And we had much to pray for.

We had been part of another church before, but its focus at the time seemed to be on the building fund. I admit that under normal circumstances we'd not only have been attentive and supportive, we'd have thrown fund-raisers for the cause ourselves. But with the fight for Terri's life at the forefront of our minds, the last thing we wanted to hear about was the status of the fund and how lovely the architectural drawings were. That's when we switched to another church.

Being honest, I admit that part of our frustration had to do with the constant reminders of the rules of the Catholic faith itself. What had once felt like familiar structure and security now began to feel cold ... almost disappointing. Once again guilt nagged at my soul. Was I rebelling only because we weren't getting what we wanted? As much as we were hoping for a miracle, I don't know if we really believed that the clouds were going to open up and deliver us one. More than anything, I think we just wanted something to comfort our souls. We needed to be able to rest our heavy load.

I suppose the angst began to show on my face, because it wasn't long before a member of the congregation suggested that I consider an upcoming silent retreat for its male members scheduled for the new year. "It's just one weekend, and it would be good for you, Robert," he said. "Sometimes we just need to shut the noise out and recharge in order to go on." I decided to consider it. Deep down I felt somewhat guilty for losing enthusiasm for the church. Everyone there had been so incredibly supportive. And yet, the echo in our souls began to grow. Why?

"I don't know, Robert," Terri finally said one day after we returned home from Mass with that lackluster feeling. "Could it be that it's because we should be saying 'thank you' instead of constantly asking for something, as we now find ourselves doing of late? Always 'please help us with this, please take care of that'? Please, please, please?"

I nodded slowly. "You mean, focus on our gratitude for what we do have instead of on the distress for what we lack?"

"Something like that," she said. "Maybe we need to just say 'thank you,' from now on. If we are to get the things that we desire most, then maybe we need to first show that we appreciate what we already have." Then she laughed. "Maybe it all boils down to simple manners."

Up to that point I had always seen us as the kind of family that appreciated the blessings we'd been showered with, the opportunities and the luxuries that came with them. But perhaps now we needed to be even more consciously grateful. And so we began focusing on gratitude in earnest. Yes, perhaps some doors were being slammed shut on us. But we would not stare at them in despair for so long that we failed to see which others had begun to inch open.

Perhaps encouraged by her attempts at more holistic healing, it was at this point that Terri began to spend a lot of time with a rather large book called *Autobiography of a Yogi* by Paramahansa Yogananda. I let her be as I always had—giving her the space she needed to let her mind journey and explore.

Editscope and its small staff continued to be part of our daily routine. I continued taking my wife out for romantic lunch dates a few times a week, always trying different restaurants and spots to keep stagnation at bay, always holding her hand, kissing her on the cheek or lightly on her lips when I could. Her muscles may have stopped moving, but that didn't mean that the world around her had to as well. We had always made sure to keep the fresh factor in our lives as high as possible before ALS. I would do so now as best I could. The practical restraints of money, however, were beginning to flex their own muscle.

Meanwhile, that steady waterfall of work that the Editscope team had been working toward had not yet cracked through the rocks. So far all we had was a trickle. It was hardly enough. As a last-ditch effort to drum up business, in November 2003 we decided to participate in a trade convention put on in Las Vegas by the National Association of Broadcasters. The entire team went, including Terri and me. We made arrangements for the boys to stay with their aunt Patty.

Las Vegas was just the distraction we needed—busy, energizing, all about the moment and forgetting what you left behind. The show felt successful in terms of contacts made, but in the end it proved to be too little, too late. While we had fun taking in the Broadway shows and soaking up the escape, in hindsight we should have walked away from the whole thing. But where hope took us, we followed. That was just the way we operated, even when on our last leg. The end of the year was on the horizon by the time it was painfully clear that we'd have to close the company's doors for good. We were preparing to file for bankruptcy.

In the weeks leading up to Christmas, Terri and I went shopping to buy a small gift for each staff member, loading up our purchases on her lap as we zipped through the mall. We couldn't afford much, but we felt we had to show our appreciation for what had been two years of good company and a much-needed daily distraction.

As usual, the time came when I had to take Terri to the ladies' room. With her going to the bathroom an average of twelve times a day, I had become an expert at the task. I almost chuckled as we approached the sign with the image of the stick lady on the door. I had by now been in so many ladies' rooms that I no longer hesitated or showed any hint of apology on my face to the unsuspecting ladies, who naturally reacted with surprise the second I made my way in. "Terri," I said one day while out at a restaurant, "I bet we're the first thing they mention about their day at the mall when they see their friends." The truth is, neither Terri nor I really cared much about how it looked to others. Illness, especially when coupled with someone you love, has a way of distinguishing between what matters and what does not.

The plan was for a holiday lunch at China Grill on Miami Beach. It would be the last time we'd be gathering as a team. Terri sat at the head of the table and handed out little poems she'd taken the time to write for each member. It was quintessential Terri at work:

We ordered a Lexus for each of you
But Kendall Toyota would not accept an IOU.
What other gift could we give in lieu?
We searched Dadeland but gift selections from Scrooges
were few.
Realizing e-mails are both free and cool,
We sent this view of the Editscope crew!

Kat
First in the line of fire,
Taking BS from customers and straight-faced liars.
Bad enough she cannot make out a word Terri is saying,
She has to daily deal with five guys crying money we ain't
making.
Graceful and smiling, she dealt with the lot,
This charming blonde who connects the dots.

Steve
Our dynamic operations manager with a vengeance against
Peachtree,
Always harassing BellSouth to get telephone service for free.
A vegetarian of highest integrity and doubtful memory.
Give him no keys or documents or they will definitely become
history.

Jon
Our tech support is definitely worth the rate,
Although Warren thinks he's illiterate.
Always with a positive mood,
This Rasta will work for food.

Pete
Part dictator, part Jack Benny,
This man guards with extreme tenacity every single Editscope
penny.
Seeking sales in the great beyond with extraordinary agility,
One thing is sure, he has never heard of humility.

Julio
A gifted artist and gentleman in every way,
Except when bugged to hell! Will Klarita be ready today?
If only Mexicans could tell north from south, east from west,
Going to Sawgrass Mall would not require a compass and
IQ test.

Eduardo
This graphics giant is getting faster,
Once a lackey but now a master.
Respect due from the Editscope clan.
As of now, the Ecuadorian is the man!

Merry Christmas
Robert and Terri

It was our way of saying "good-bye and thank you." That we
would miss them, we had no doubt. That we were now faced with
growing financial burdens was also another obvious nagging sore
on the skin.

Meanwhile, Terri's symptoms persisted. Other than regaining peristalsis, which technically had more to do with physical inactivity than ALS itself, she had not seen any improvement to her overall condition.

That New Year's Eve night, we headed out to a friend's house for a private party that promised to entertain some two hundred friends and acquaintances. It was to be a casual but elegant affair in a grand home, set on a sprawling lot in the farming district south of where we lived.

By then word had gotten around that Terri indeed had Lou Gehrig's disease. We were not denying it, of course—we never had—we just didn't want others to dwell on it, especially if they felt obliged to say something helpful just for the sake of it. We understood that most were well-intentioned, and we acknowledged that there were no companion manuals for unhappy and socially uncomfortable situations like these. But I knew that Terri didn't like the word *sick* attributed to her. I hoped that our friends would somehow know to avoid the word or the sentiment altogether without my having to send out a memo. She didn't want their pity. Compassion, yes. A "poor Terri" approach, no. Sometimes a long, tight hug and a smile was all she craved from others … just an acknowledgment that she was going through a challenge, with a reminder that she was not battling it out alone. A loving army—even a small one—is often the tonic one needs when facing an enemy only you can battle.

The long, narrow driveway was beautifully lined with torches. As we pulled up closer to the house, other guests were walking through the front door, their faces lit up in anticipation of a good night ahead. The night sky was clear, giving center stage to the half moon above that sat like a carefully hung lantern. That night Terri had chosen to wear a pair of easy slacks and a pretty floral blouse. I had taken her to her longtime hairdresser earlier that day. I wanted her to feel beautiful and confident. While dressing her that evening, however, I had sensed some tension. I asked if she wanted to skip the outing, assuring her that it was quite fine if we chose not to go. With Editscope's pending bankruptcy coming at us in the new year, I felt only half-hearted about ringing in what I knew was going to be a rough year. It wasn't that I was embarrassed about our situation—I'd been on the bone of my ass before and survived—but sometimes putting on that brave smile required more energy than you could muster.

But she declined with a single turn of her head. "No, I'm okay … let's take a breeze out and see our friends," she said. "It's New Year's Eve. And since when have we ever passed up a good party?" I knew she had not yet completely emerged from her depression, but I could tell that she was trying hard. I kissed her on the forehead. Tonight would not be the first time we'd be socializing since her symptoms had intensified, but certainly the first time in a much larger setting, where not everyone was a close friend.

As we made our way to the front door, we could hear the music and excited voices coming from within the house. We smiled as we greeted everyone along our path. Those who knew us immediately halted their conversations or left their chairs to welcome us. Acquaintances smiled politely and did their best not to stare or be seen as inquisitive.

It really was everything anyone could hope for in a happy gathering such as this—a beautiful home looking like something out of a high-end decor magazine, set in its own tropical foliage forest; incredible music; warm company; and fabulous fare with top-shelf champagne being poured everywhere you looked. Around us, smiles and laughter cut into the cool night air like never-ending mini fireworks. For a moment, I allowed myself to sink into the old familiar vibe of happier times when we had everything to smile about—when we were the ones hosting a happy event such as this, greeting friends with hugs and smiles into our home. The blessings—they had indeed been many. Caught up in the moment, I lifted Terri out of her chair, held her up with my arms, and allowed her feet to rest on mine. And for a brief spell, we were just another couple on the dance floor enjoying the music, the party, and each other, face-to-face.

I don't know exactly what triggered it or how long it had been swelling inside her. Maybe Terri, too, had allowed herself to remember what that life had once felt like ... what it was like to dance so hard she'd have to wipe the sweat off her brow or kick her shoes off so she could really throw herself into it ... collapse into the nearest seat because she'd just gone for an hour without a break. Maybe she went back to that time when our worries were of a different kind—the normal kind. I don't know. But at some point after midnight, Terri burst into tears. I hurried over to find our host kneeling next to her, holding her hands in his and clearly doing his best to console her. He had been kind enough to pull her over to the side for some privacy. His show of compassion was enough to make my eyes water. My heart felt like it was being ripped in two. I thanked my friend for his swift thinking and big heart. It could not have been easy to do. I mean, what do you *really* say to someone who's falling apart because they're dying? Hang in there? Stay strong? That's life? Looking back, I appreciate that it had to have been one of the hardest conversations our friend ever had.

Terri never did speak about it afterward. To be frank, I didn't ask. Really, there was no point to it. Some things simply don't require a conversation. She was brave enough as it was to show up and sit there, knowing full well that while her life had already been served notice, energy pulsated in the cells of every other body that surrounded her that night. And all she could do was watch as the music made their limbs and muscles do what hers no longer could.

The pain you feel today is the strength you feel tomorrow. For every challenge encountered there is opportunity for growth.

—Ritu Ghatourey

CHAPTER 12

Even in a Storm Lies a Center of Calm

The year 2004 came at us like the bad dream we'd been anticipating. The company in which we'd invested money and hope was officially declaring bankruptcy. With Wassi Art still struggling, I took a hard look at our situation to see where I could find some financial wiggle room. I had a family to support.

"Terri," I said to her one morning soon after the company had finished filing the necessary papers. I squeezed her hand and lowered my head slightly before continuing. "I don't know how to tell you this, honey, but we may have to change course for a while."

She nodded. "Money."

"Yes. It's getting tight now. I'm so sorry … I don't think we can hold on for much longer as is. The lease on the apartment will end shortly, so maybe now's a good a time as any to call it a day. We need to save what we can until we're on better footing."

She nodded. "I'll talk to Patty and see if it's okay for us to stay with her again for a bit. I'm sure she'll understand."

I knelt before her. "I'm sorry," I said, burying my face in her chest. I hugged her close. "This is all my fault for not taking care of things differently. I should have done better."

"No. Not your fault, Robert. Life. Just life. We didn't see this coming. How could we?"

I had many reasons for adoring my wife as I did. Not being a fair-weather friend was one. She never berated me for making mistakes, and she accepted our bumps in the road with grace, including those of the financial kind. She understood that I was human and, therefore, fallible.

My life was spiraling out of control. I felt winded. Dizzy. Disoriented. Sometimes when I went to get the kids from school or to the supermarket, I'd stop at the church and just sit there like a scared kid, praying to God for help, the tears pouring down my face. Except that I was a man, a grown man—one with children of his own to raise and a wife who was getting sicker by the day. Where do grown men go when we're the ones who are frightened and confused? We're supposed to be the strong ones. Who props us up when we're weak? We're expected to have all the answers. To whom do we turn when we have none? I never told Terri about these moments, nor anyone else for that matter. I stood alone in a fog that had swallowed me whole.

It wasn't that I doubted I could care for my wife. But the weight of being a man in charge when things were falling apart was now more than I could bear. My children were suffering. My financial picture had more fissures than a desert rock. I needed to find hope again. Comfort. Something. A miracle. Or a safe harbor to rest my soul for just one day. At this point I'd take any crumb I could find.

In the end I decided that I would join the silent retreat being offered by our church. It would be one of the last times I reached out to organized religion for comfort.

And so for one weekend, I gathered with twenty-five or so other men from our church in a dormitory in Miami. We met to pray, to meditate, and to listen to words of inspiration and encouragement from others who had walked similar paths of fear, uncertainty, and hopelessness. There were rules to abide by. The only time we were allowed to speak was between the hours of 10:00 a.m. and 12:00 p.m. That's when we each took turns giving our testimonials, "getting out there" whatever it was that was troubling our souls. The goal was to learn how to handle whatever it was that was causing us to stare into the darkness at nights while the rest of the world slumbered.

"My wife has ALS," I started, when it was my turn. "It's a terminal neurological disease. The doctors say she won't have much longer to live. Most only survive two to five years. I don't know how to help my children cope with it now, much less when her time comes. I don't know how I'll keep my family afloat. But, more than anything, I don't know how I'm going to live without her. To be honest, I still haven't accepted the fact that she may really die. I'm still praying for that miracle."

It was as simple as that. As I said the words, it occurred to me that it was the first time I was actually sharing my burden with other human beings. It sounds odd to say, but even though these gentlemen were strangers to me, I felt as if I was in the company of close friends. I listened as others did their best to get past the tightness in their throats and limited eye contact to share their own testimonials. We listened. Those of us who were able to offer words of comfort, did. At the end, none of us got handed a miracle in a bag, but the very simple and human process of sharing with others was more helpful than I could have imagined. I was happy I went. But the gathering of souls was not the most significant part of that weekend. In my devotion to silence, I got the lifeline that I had most longed for. It was from Terri herself.

She had slipped a short letter into my overnight bag. I found it on my first night. This is what my wife said to me:

Dear Robert,

I hope you are getting some much-needed rest and that your retreat is providing you with a fresh and deep spiritual renewal.

We have been through so much together for the past thirteen years that there is very little we don't know of each other or of things we have not said to each other. My illness is taking its toll on you. Yet the more sick and clumsy I get, the more you tell me you love me. Sometimes I am not sure that I deserve such love.

You undertake your task of husband, dad, mom, caregiver, cook, maid, and chauffeur with a willingness, joy, and perfection that sometimes make it easy for us to take it for granted. I don't want to be sick, but being sick I think God chose you above all others to be there for the kids and me. God's probably as happy with you as I am with His choice.

I do not know what lies ahead for us, but with you all things seem possible. I am glad you have a deep love for our Lord. It keeps my faith strong too and grounds our kids.

The most endearing quality about you is your innocence. You still get excited about things and are always the eternal optimist even at the worst times. You cry; you hug. You say I am wrong, I am sorry, I am lost.

I love you, Robert. You are a good person and a wonderful Christian man. I pray God to bless you and strengthen you always.

Love and kisses,
Terri
P.S. Hurry home! I need food! ☺

The letter from my beloved wife, the caress of her words, her attention to my soul, her acknowledgment of how I felt, and the pain I was also enduring—they all made my heart ache even further for an end to her illness. It took an incredible act of selflessness for her to put aside her own nightmare just to give me—a healthy person with a whole life ahead of me—the support she knew I needed. For that I loved her even more. Hers was all the encouragement I wanted.

It was all I needed.

When the lease was finally up, we prepared to move. The sight of the brown cardboard boxes was now a somewhat familiar one, and I wondered what effect the instability of our home was having on Alex and Justin.

When I was a young kid growing up, my parents had sent my siblings and me to boarding school before we were even ten years old. Their intentions were in the right place—a good education was their primary concern, and school in the countryside was extremely limited. We had all survived the experience, of course, but I had always promised myself that I would do my best to stick close to my children if I could help it. I had managed to do that with our two boys throughout their mom's illness, but still I worried about them. I just knew they had to be harboring feelings of fear and confusion, even resentment. Perhaps it was a mistake, but I used their performance at school as a yardstick for their ability to handle it all. As they were doing fairly well, I talked myself into believing that they were okay. It was a lie I desperately needed to believe.

When we moved back to Patty's, I did some light renovations to the second bathroom so as to compensate for the tight squeeze and imposition we were putting my sister-in-law through once again. I can't say we had grown accustomed to our nomadic life, but we had learned how to roll with it. Deep down, however, Terri and I knew this was going to be another temporary arrangement.

Amid the boxes and gentle chaos at Patty's, we kept our focus and continued with Terri's stretches, massages, and raw food diet. One day, while searching the Internet for more raw food recipes, we came across a video featuring an international raw food chef by the name of Aris Latham. We immediately ordered a copy. A couple days later our purchase arrived, and we settled in front of the television to watch. Within minutes, familiar panoramic scenes flashed across the screen. The video had been filmed in Jamaica. A few scenes later, we burst out laughing. The platters and bowls being used were none other than Wassi creations. On closer inspection of the video's jacket, we realized that the producers were acquaintances of ours. We took it as a sign. So when the boys' summer holiday break came around, we packed our suitcases and headed back to our island.

This trip would end up differently, however. With no home, no prospects in Miami for income, and no real treatment available for Terri, we decided that while we would send Alex back to Miami in August to begin high school, Terri, Justin, and I would remain in Jamaica for the year. Maybe with our being there, business would improve. And if luck was on our side, perhaps we'd be able to sell a piece of property we still had left. At this point, we had nothing to lose.

Perhaps it was too much to ask of our young sons, strong and resilient as they were. Alex would have to go through the critical stage of high school without his parents to come home to daily. Justin was leaving a school system and friends he had come to know. Terri and I hated the sacrifice our boys had to make. More than anything, it sat heavy on our hearts that we were splitting up the family. The guilt was our constant companion, but at the time we could think of no other option. I just needed a chance to breathe and find my next foothold. I told myself it was temporary. I would not know how the boys really felt until it was all behind us:

Was I resentful over the fact that I was more or less left on my own? In hindsight, yes, more than I wanted to admit. I struggled with it. At first I dealt with it by spending hours at the arcade, then with friends as I grew older and could get away on my own. I felt guilty for being angry about it and had to remind myself that Mom was sick. She couldn't walk, and seemed to be getting sicker. As time went on, she could do less and less for herself. The worse she got, the more I pulled away. I thought that maybe if I didn't see it, then it wouldn't exist. It would go away. Then there was Dad. I got that his position was a tough one. It was either choose to focus on raising us and put Mom in a home, or choose to take care of Mom himself and have Justin and me fit around the situation. Deep down I know I'd have absolutely hated it if we had put Mom in a home with total strangers looking after her while she waited for us to visit. She didn't belong there. I didn't want that for her either. She deserved to be with us. Her family. But, at the same time, it was confusing as a kid knowing that at the end of the day you had to take a backseat to your parents. I wasn't sure how to handle it, to be honest. Either way, it was what it was. And there was absolutely nothing we could do about it. Our hands were just as tied as Mom was stuck in her wheelchair.

—Alex

As soon as we settled in again, I got help with caring for Terri from a couple of our former housekeepers, with my supervision never far away. I admit I was relieved. The extra hands gave me a chance to breathe a little. Now I had time to do simple things like take a walk to clear my head, read the newspaper cover to cover, or sip at my coffee slowly instead of flushing it down my throat. Terri kept encouraging me to take even more time to reconnect with family and friends. And so I did, but only in short spurts. I knew she was concerned about my own state of mind and the worries I carried about our financial situation. But the ladies who were now caring for Terri still needed my help. They didn't quite know how to make her comfortable. They could tell by the grimace on her face, or the sounds she made, that they were hurting her. It made me realize just how much she had come to depend on me.

Meanwhile, I had already managed to locate chef Aris Latham through a few friends, and I told Terri I'd meet with him and see if I couldn't persuade him to come to the house to show us a few recipes.

Terri continued to follow her new holistic lifestyle, quietly journeying deeper into Eastern philosophy. She had by now completed reading *Autobiography of a Yogi*, and placed it in my hands with the suggestion that I read it.

"It makes sense to me, Robert, the whole approach to spirituality. It feels right. Especially now. I think this is it for me. I'm not abandoning religion," she explained. "I still believe in God, but I no longer want to go to church. Right now I need something more … much more. Something to add to what we already know. Church with all its rules … it no longer fulfills me. Now I need something I can participate in without having to show up at a particular building at a particular time. I hope you understand."

I told her I wanted whatever made her happy. And I meant it. I started reading the book that night. In the end I didn't complete it, but I read enough to at least understand where Terri was headed. She was now looking within.

One night, she broached a topic that had long been on her mind. I had just bathed her and finished putting a pillow under her knees to ease the pressure on her back. I rubbed her feet a little before lying next to her to watch the evening news.

"Robert," she said, in a way that signaled what she was about to say required my full attention. I turned down the volume. Outside, beyond the louver windows, the crickets sang into the night sky. "Robert, I want you to know that it's okay."

"What's okay, honey? What do you mean?" She paused and looked down for a second before looking at me again. This time her voice came back softly.

"To ... to see other women. I wouldn't and couldn't blame you. Under the circumstances, I mean."

I sat up and held her hand. She looked into my eyes, bracing for the hurt that she had anticipated might come. I won't deny that during the course of my wife's illness, temptation had presented itself to me from time to time. And I won't deny that there were moments when I had to will myself to turn and walk away from it. The thing is that, despite my deep love for my wife, I was still human. The yearning for "normalcy" is ever present. No matter how well you're coping with a hardship, the life you had before the chaos is a dream you wish you could touch for even a moment. I quickly came to see how others in my position might succumb to an escape to soothe their own wounds, particularly if their spouse has shown no or little appreciation for their efforts to care for them. Appreciation is not often forthcoming from one who is in constant physical or emotional pain. Impatience, bitterness, and resentment more often trump all else when your life has been forever changed by illness.

I was lucky. I knew that Terri appreciated everything I did for her. Yes, she had her moments of frustration, but then I'd always remind myself that I was not the one with a terminal illness. I was healthy—at least for the time being. So I chose to not cross that line. I just didn't want to. I assured my wife that I was not going to take her up on her generous offer. "No, Terri. I'm not about to do that. I'm committed to you in every way. I'm not stepping out of this marriage for a few cheap thrills just because of ALS. Besides, we're still able to be intimate. Our love life is still great! So what more could I possibly want?"

But she continued as if she hadn't heard me. "I know how it is with men. I would understand if—"

"No. Listen to me. Why would I make all this sacrifice to look after you, only to then turn around and spoil it all on something—or someone—that means nothing to me? Why?"

She gave me a guarded smile. "Okay. I just wanted to say it out loud in case the thought had crossed your mind. Wanted you to know that it had crossed mine too."

"My family's happiness is all that matters to me, Terri. I'm still in love with my children's mother. End of discussion. Banish the thought from your mind." And we never did talk about it again.

It was already September. By now Alex had already returned to school in Miami. We kept in constant touch with our son—I, usually by phone, and Terri by e-mail so that she could be better understood. We knew he was being well cared for by family, but that only took the edge off the guilt we felt for having left him behind.

Hi Mom and Dad,

I'm glad to hear you guys are doing well. I'm doing a bit better in school now. The problem with my algebra teacher is being solved, so I really don't have any more problems with it. Happy to hear from you. Just replying to let you know I got your e-mail!

Love,
Alex

My dearest Son,

I am so happy to hear from you. Finally, after two long years, you got your computer. Dad tells me it's a nice one too. Great! It makes us happy when you are happy. Now don't forget your homework, okay?

Life is a bit on the quiet side, but we don't mind as we have had our fair share of excitement. We are busy organizing Wassi Art. We don't have long hours anymore or work on the weekends like we used to. I have learned from my mistakes. It seems next year will be a great year for both Wassi and the family.

My new nickname is now "Queenbee," since everyone here is trying to take care of me. This has made life a bit easier for Dad. Money is tight for now, but we are happy, especially with you not mad at us anymore. Looking forward to seeing you in December.

Lots of love,
Mom

I can say now that while we knew separating the family was far from ideal, neither Terri nor I fully understood the pain and confusion the boys were going through. It is, to this day, one of my deepest regrets.

Meanwhile, I continued to attack our finances from all the angles I could think of. But with the country in an even deeper recession, nothing seemed to be working. A friend had suggested taking a stab at an importation business. Everyone he knew in that line of business was doing well, he said. It made sense. The only problem was that it meant taking a business trip to China to establish contacts and get it going. I told him I'd have to think about it.

While I had my mind on a potential trip to the Far East, another issue was brewing off the coast of Africa. In the days that led to its eventual arrival late on the night of September 11 and the early morning of September 12, Hurricane Ivan grew in size and brawn to become a strong category four storm. Its eerie timing did not go unnoticed—exactly sixteen years earlier, category five Hurricane Gilbert had crushed the island as if it were nothing more than a cheap tin can. This time the island's citizens displayed no bravado. They prepared ... and cowered.

That night, as Ivan loomed in the darkness toward the south coast of the island, Terri, Justin, and I huddled together in our bedroom. The electricity had already been cut throughout most of the island. Outside, the winds from the storm's outer bands had begun to howl and scream as they lunged across the island. I told my family we'd be okay and smiled reassuringly, but I secretly worried about the possibility of having to move quickly with Terri should the roof become compromised. I said my prayers silently over and over again, wondering if this was how it was going to end for us.

And then it happened. Now just within miles of striking the island's south coast and swallowing whole the heavily populated capital city of Kingston, Ivan swung a hard left as if suddenly distracted by something in its peripheral view. He lumbered to the west, sparing the island a crippling blow. It was nothing short of a miracle.

In the weeks and months that followed Ivan, business boomed only for those that dealt with the essentials—food and pharmaceuticals. As we rang in the year 2005, we prepared ourselves for much of the same. Not surprisingly, sales at Wassi continued to soften. I acknowledged the situation and told myself that I couldn't afford to let that stop me. I continued searching for a suitable exit. But there were no buyers in the market for just any kind of ongoing business, especially ones that were barely treading water. The property we had was now officially up for sale, and while there were good prospects buzzing around, waiting for the right one to land would take time. And time was not something we had in surplus. I suppose in the back of my mind I knew I could turn to my family for help. But I wanted to avoid the imposition. Everyone had his burden to bear.

Terri and I quietly held our breaths, praying for some good news. In April we indulged in a surprise distraction. Dr. Deepak Chopra was scheduled to appear as the honored guest speaker for a charity event in Kingston. I knew that Terri had long admired the esteemed celebrity author and spiritual teacher. So I made the arrangements with the charity's chairman to have her meet him. On the evening of the grand gala, Dr. Chopra sat alone with Terri for a few minutes. And in the short time he had with her, he assured his devoted student that she was giving ALS a most incredible and beautiful fight.

I kept hitting every prospective buyer I could see, smell, or sense in the distance. Refusing to worry, I maintained my calm composure, sending out repeated messages to the universe that my family needed some good news. And at the eleventh hour, just when I thought I had exhausted all avenues, we found that elusive buyer.

A few months later we returned to Miami.

I cried that I had no shoes. And then I
met a man who had no feet.

—Old Persian Proverb

CHAPTER 13

Pulling Back from the Brink

With the housing market being somewhat in our favor, that year we were able to find another reasonable purchase in the Hammocks area, close by the boys' schools. Out came the boxes once again.

After settling in, we immediately resumed Terri's massage sessions with Patty, and Pilates therapy sessions with Brent Anderson. This time around, Brent suggested we take it a step further. There was a specialty therapist on Florida's west coast by the name of Aaron Mattes. A household name amongst professional athletes, including top names such as Carl Lewis, Mattes had developed a system of correcting injuries caused by trauma or even neurological disease. His technique involved the stretching of muscles in isolation. He called it active isolated stretching, or AIS. Terri and I immediately lit up. Maybe he could get Terri's muscles moving again.

Before long we were sitting face-to-face with the soft-spoken Mattes. He explained his theory and technique with great patience, respect, and encouragement. In the end, however, with the three-hour-long drive being a stretch of a different kind, we consulted with him only twice so he could show me how to manipulate Terri's fingers, arms, and legs. Our goal was to reduce

145

her spasticity somewhat. The spasticity had become increasingly hard on her, particularly at night while she was trying to sleep. As she was unable to move on her own to switch positions, sleeping the night through was fast becoming a luxury of the past. I'd begun to wake up not once or twice, but several times during the night to help her change the position of her body, massage her legs, and take her to the bathroom.

Mattes never made any promises, of course—no one did after the official diagnosis was delivered. But his therapy and help gave us some hope that we might be able to delay the final outcome or, at the very least, make her life that much more bearable.

By now Terri's detoxification was in full swing. She had made no exceptions to her consumption of organic raw foods while in Jamaica. Her almost reborn skin was proof that her body was benefiting from the effort. She had stuck to her three-part program like a champion; cleansed her colon, liver, and kidneys; and continued with acupuncture, massages, and daily stretching. She had eliminated all forms of processed foods from her diet, and she kept up with every herbal remedy she could find. She had even purchased a book on Chinese medicine that dealt with cleansing the blood through certain herbs and foods. Whatever was out there to be tried, we stuck our fingers in it.

The result was a new Terri. Her skin now had the glow and suppleness of that of a young girl. Friends who had not seen her in the year we were away noticed the difference immediately, and they peered at her in amazement. While Terri had always had a beautiful complexion, now she looked astoundingly radiant. It made her status as a terminally ill patient all the more heart-wrenching ... confusing.

"But, Terri, you actually look *younger*," some would marvel.

"How is this even possible?" others would ask.

"You look so healthy! Does this mean you're getting better?"

That, of course, was the question to which we didn't have the answer. The truth is that while she may have looked better on the outside, on the inside ALS continued its mission to claim her body. Her fingers were the disease's latest conquest. Now already beginning to curl, they could barely hold a cup or a fork ... or just about anything, for that matter.

The worst part was that it was now impacting the one thing she needed more than anything to feel human and purposeful— the ability to communicate. Using a pen or keyboard now required that much more effort. And yet, my wife and the mother of our children never lost the focus she needed to be an active member of our family. Through her short scribbles, she continued to run our household:

Alex, please don't shout at Justin. Lowers self-esteem.

Robert, think Justin has bronchitis. Soon pneumonia. Take him somewhere to clear lungs. Buy nebulizer mask at pharmacy.

Make smoothie for boys. Goji berries, cranberry juice, pine, sweet pepper, lettuce, cucumber, bee pollen, honey, banana. Good for them.

Buy nuts for coffee table.

She also continued to be in charge of her own care:

Put on buy list: Psyllium fiber, rug tape so cushion stop sliding. Put towel on chair so butt hurts less.

Lymph system removes waste from body. Lymph work only when body moves.

Not sick! Annoy me when say sick!

And other times she just had a request for herself:

Please play old songs. "Unchained Melody." "You've
Lost That Loving Feeling."

But that wasn't all. As if losing the use of her fingers and
hands wasn't cruel enough, her speech had also reached the point
of being nothing more than shapeless sounds. I was now the
only one on the entire planet with whom she could make herself
understood—the only one. The disease, for all our consulting;
all our researching; all the diets, therapies, techniques, and
procedures we tried was still driving forward. It was as if our
efforts were nothing more than minor objects of debris in the
road. No matter what we threw at it, all ALS did was find a way
around it.

When I say that I began to worry about Terri, understand that
I was already sick with grief over her diagnosis and the thought
of her being in any amount of pain or even discomfort. What I
mean to say, I suppose, is that now I felt that she was beginning
to slip away in more ways than the obvious.

Sometime after we returned to Miami, I made the decision
to attend the trade show in southern China. We were in better
financial shape now, but I figured that if I could start another
business to help shore us up, then it would be worth the try. I
discussed it with Terri first and asked if she would be okay with
my going. It would mean a two-week absence, the longest we'd
be apart since her diagnosis. Would she be okay with it if we got
Patty to stay with her? Not surprisingly, she not only told me to
go, she assured me it would all be fine. Weeks later, I was at a
trade show in southern China.

Unfortunately, the trip didn't go as planned. After taking numerous calls a day from Patty, I decided it was best to cut it short and return home. I could hardly focus on anything I was doing there. Looking after Terri had turned out to be more than anyone or even two caregivers could handle. I can't say I was surprised. I had become a one-man team and had put in much time learning exactly how to turn her this way, move her that way, prop her head just so. Anyone else could only hope to be a distant understudy.

The minute I returned, I could see on Terri's face that she was unhappy. Not unhappy that I had left her, but unhappy about something else. Her smile, while plain to see on her lips, had slipped away from her eyes. What was troubling her, exactly, she didn't share with me. But she was clearly distant. I kept asking her what was wrong, but she'd only shake her head and produce a smile. To be honest, I felt stupid for forcing the issue. Who wouldn't feel melancholy in the face of a terminal illness?

I returned to my life of caring for my wife 'round the clock. Before long I was waking up in the mornings feeling as if I hadn't slept at all. My eyes burned from the moment I opened them. Now I caught myself constantly yawning, splashing cold water on my face, and rubbing my aching back and neck. I felt the weight around my middle hang like an appendage. I needed to exercise. I found myself dreaming about running, but I didn't want to leave Terri more than was absolutely necessary. I admit now that there was more to it. In a way, I felt that doing something only a healthy person could do was a reminder of her plight. She didn't need that. And I certainly didn't want to be the one to rub it in her face. But, still, the life that was once mine flickered in my mind every now and then. It's not that we were recluses. That would not happen for another few years. But we were getting there.

Then, one day, the pivot that I needed took place. With the boys already at school, I was in the family room trying to relax for a bit, watching the morning news, enjoying my first cup of coffee. I had already taken Terri to the bathroom, washed her face, brushed her hair, dressed her, and made her smoothie. I can't say what the news item was that had me distracted, but I remember suddenly noticing that she was no longer in the room watching along with me. That in and of itself was not unusual. She had a motorized chair and had the run of the house. But something told me to go find her. I got up immediately.

Within seconds I spotted her in front of the computer. Her back to me, she sat perfectly still, clearly lost in whatever it was she was reading. I smiled, already relaxing in the knowledge that she was perfectly fine, just entertaining herself on the Internet as she often did. I almost returned to the television but decided to go and give her a quick kiss. And that's when I saw the computer screen. She was researching ways to commit suicide. I quickly spun her chair around and fell to my knees.

"Terri!" I held her face in my hands so she had to look at me. Her eyes had already closed as if to shut me out. "Honey, what are you doing?"

She shook her head, her eyes still squeezed shut. A low sound escaped her throat. I could not even make it out. It was as if her tongue was sitting completely still like a lead slab while the words she tried to form worked their way around it.

I felt my heart tear away from my chest. For the first time I understood that my wife was living with the knowledge that her death was imminent. It wasn't some intellectual reality tucked away far below the horizon. It was already in her line of sight and moving toward her. She was giving up. Had it been anyone else, I'd have expected it. But this was Terri. The woman who looked fear in the face and still found a way to make her mouth curl up at the corners. The woman who had come up with her own theory and plan to rejuvenate herself. And who had stuck to it long enough to see the results.

I pulled her in and hugged her hard. "No, Terri. Don't you be thinking like this now. Not you, honey. We need you! You know we do! Who's going to help me make all the tough decisions? We're not a complete family without you. Don't you know how much we want you here?" I pulled away to let her see the smile on my face. I admit it was more of a plea in disguise. A few tears fell as she opened her eyes. I brushed them away with a soft kiss. "Honey, I'm here for you! I know you suffer. That's why I'm here. Please believe me. I see you. I see your reality every day."

She tried again to speak. It didn't even sound like her. I shook my head. "It's okay, Terri. You don't have to—"

But this time she shook her head and held up her hand. I rested on my heels as she tried again. She pointed to herself and shook her head. Then she pointed at me and nodded.

"I don't understand, honey. What do you mean?"

Again she pointed at me. "You ... good man. Good husband. Tired."

"But, honey, I'm okay, I promise you!"

The tears filled her eyes again as she struggled to say more. Just watching her suffer the frustration of not being able to speak even a single word clearly was enough to make my heart race.

"Burden."

"Burden? What do you mean?"

She turned to the computer and moved her chair in. This time she typed out the rest.

"Robert. This has nothing to do with me. I know I am sick whether I want to say it out loud or not. I know that I am dying, one limb at a time. I wish nothing more than to be well again

151

and to have my life back. To live. I want to live. But what hurts me more than anything else is to know that I am now a burden to you. I see that you can no longer live your life. I know how that must make you feel since mine has already been cut in half and has me reduced to this wheelchair. The difference is, you are able-bodied and can still do everything you want. I am the reason you don't do the things that bring you joy. The little and the big things. I'm the reason you don't do what you need to for the boys. For the family. I'm in the way. I'm the problem. That's why I need to go. I just can't continue much longer like this. Watching your lives unravel because of me."

I remained on my knees. "Terri, listen to me. You have to stop thinking like this. Put out of your mind that any of this is a burden. Please, honey."

She turned back to the computer and put her hands over the keyboard. "Then would you at least consult with an attorney and find out if there are legal ways in which to do this? To commit suicide? I need to know. I may get worse, Robert. Think about that. A lot worse. For all of us."

And it was then that I understood. If I were to give Terri my full commitment to look after her, really be her caregiver in every sense of the word, really convince her that I wanted to do this for her, then I'd have to stop trying to live my life while caring for her at the same time. There was no possibility of having it both ways. I would have to lock away into a mental box everything that I wanted for myself. Everything I desired. This was my job now. One of my own choosing. I would have to give her not just all my time, but my dreams, my hopes, and my love. It would have to be a certain kind of unbreakable, unconditional love that would stand strong and happy in the face of any emotion or fatigue that was yet to come. It would have to be the selfless kind that you put squarely behind someone who needs it. And I knew of only one kind of love that fit the description. It was the kind of love that only a mother could give.

A mother's love.

When I saw this plaque at Baptist Hospital in Miami, I felt each word sink into my weary heart.

—Robert

To the Caregivers of the World

God looked down from above,
And in an act of perfect love
He chose you above the rest
To carry out His greatest test.
He chose you to bravely bear
The burden of your loved one's care.

"Why me?" perplexed you ask.
"Am I capable of such a task?
I cannot cause the road to bend.
I cannot stem the downward trend."
"Yes, but you can call from deep inside
An inner strength to slow the tide.

If you can make him smile
Forget his pain a little while
Perhaps invent some little way
To comfort him and make his day
More bright ... and tell him that you see
His courage, strength and dignity.

So when you're called upon
To do those many, many things,
Remember ... He chose you
To be God's Angel ... earning wings!"

—Unknown

CHAPTER 14

You're Stronger than You Know

I had, for the most part until now, turned to no one close to me whenever I felt the need for emotional support. It wasn't about pride. I didn't have a problem admitting when I needed help. But I had long survived on the approach that everything would be all right in the end.

The human spirit is strong, I always used to preach. You can be happy if you really want to be. It might require some work, but you can absolutely find it in yourself. And when you do, you owe it to humanity to pass it on by uplifting someone else who's having a hard time of it. You never know what the people next to you are going through. You never know what's behind the mask they wear. So you do your best to make them smile. Feel the joy. Do this, and it'll all come back full circle to prop you up just when you need it. That had always been my way. So I suppose I just thought I could handle the battle ALS had waged on our family.

Terri's thoughts of suicide changed all that for me—at least initially. It was an aberration of living that I couldn't process. I felt as if my own legs could no longer hold me up and that my lungs held no air. It was one thing to know that her death would come naturally. Yes, that alone made me want to fall to my knees and beg God for a miracle. But knowing that she was in such a dark, hopeless place that she would take her end into her own hands … well, that made me want to barter with the devil. It was one thing for ALS to take her life. It was quite another for it to destroy the very spirit that made Terri the human being she was. I knew then that my decision to look after her myself was the right choice. Had I just thrown money at her illness by putting her in a home, she would not have wanted to live a second longer. I was going to make her feel purposeful to her last breath. I loved her. And the best way to show love to someone is to be present—really present. Not thinking about yesterday or tomorrow, but today. Right now.

For days I walked around with a sick knot in my stomach, very careful now to hide from Terri any signs of my own fatigue. But one morning, after another night of interrupted sleep, I looked in the mirror and saw the face of someone I didn't recognize. My eyes were there, but now they looked hollow. Lifeless.

Later on, while she was being massaged and stretched by Patty, I went out to see my niece Rosanne and her husband. Rosanne said she knew from the moment she opened the door that I was broken:

Robert had come to visit with us as he and Terri had always done, even after the disease had really taken over. They were both quite good about not letting her illness stop them from living. Others would have called it quits immediately and just waited for the slow death to arrive. Not them. They always did their best to socialize as much as they could, and usually with a sincere effort at enjoying the moment. Terri was strong that way. She'd say that as long as she woke up, it was a good day. And those weren't just platitudes. She meant it. Even as the ALS advanced, she never publicly engaged in self-pity, never made you feel uncomfortable in her presence, never made you look for a quick excuse to find someone else to talk with. And that's the truth. Mind you, it didn't stop you from feeling sorry for her. She didn't want pity—but you couldn't help that, although it always came with admiration. I don't know how she did it, how she managed to smile and ask how *you* were doing ... but then again she had always been the hard-core optimist.

I was Robert's niece but also his peer, as we were close in age. So I had known him pretty much all my life. He was one of those exceptional individuals—always positive. Consistently happy. It was rare that you left his presence feeling anything but better about life and yourself. There was never an agenda behind it, either. It was just pure and selfless love, a genuine reaching out to a friend, or even a stranger. He had always had that kind of energy for people, you know? He made the time. Put out the effort in an honest, trusting way without a single thought to what he'd get in return. He viewed it important as a member of the human race to live this way. He focused on whomever it was he was speaking to, as if that person was the only one who mattered. For him it was the kind thing to do—the only way to be. That's just how he lived.

But that afternoon, the second I opened the door and saw him standing there, I knew he had come for more than just some company and conversation. I had not seen him in weeks, so the dark circles under his eyes were the first place mine went to. He managed to greet me with a smile—but then Robert did that for anyone no matter what. Not smiling at someone for him was tantamount to not saying "hello." Still, I knew he was off. His shoulders now slumped forward. His stride was sluggish as if his legs had doubled in weight. It was like looking at someone you knew, but this time in a skin of a different kind. I hugged him and led him to where my husband was in our family room.

At first we chatted—about what, I don't remember. But that only lasted a few minutes before the tears filled his eyes. I had to wipe away my own. It was the first time I'd seen him like this since ALS was first mentioned. Correction. It was the first time I'd seen him like this, period. We didn't ask him what was wrong. Under the circumstances, that seemed like a pretty silly question. I mean, what do you say to someone going through this kind of hell? You're sorry? They already know that. Offer solutions? There aren't any. You'll be okay? No—that's empty. So you don't really say anything. You just listen as he talks. Just be there.

I'll be honest. It's hard to watch a strong man weep. You know he's only human, but when the happiest person you know breaks like that, it becomes clear that all is not well with the universe. But that day, Robert's tears were not about him. It was for his wife and the fact that she had given up and was depressed. The hard work didn't bother him, he told us. He'd happily accepted it as his job and was at peace with that. But to know that her spirit had been broken ... to him that was like sucking the air out of his lungs.

The truth is, while we all loved Robert and Terri, most just didn't understand why he insisted on taking care of her himself. No question about it—we admired him for it. But when we tried to imagine ourselves in the same position, we just shook our heads and said "impossible." The men in particular. So to say he had the full support of his family and friends would be an exaggeration. Maybe that got to him somewhat, but I don't really think so. He wasn't one to waste too much time caring about what others thought. And for the most part, he did seem happy. They both did, actually. One thing I knew for sure was that ALS made their already strong marriage a virtual fortress. The love that flowed between them had always been palpable. Now, at least to those of us on the outside, it was almost electric. You saw it in the big picture, yes, that he was physically taking care of her. I mean, he would literally lift her to carry her anywhere the wheelchair could not go—like to the toilet, for instance. He'd scoop her up with both arms, put her on the seat, position her legs, then hold her up so she wouldn't fall over. He thought of everything. Always make sure her neck was able to rest back comfortably. Made sure she got her daily stretches and massages. He was on it like a manager.

But as a woman, I saw his thoughtfulness through the little things. He paid attention and made sure she was comfortable in a language that only women understood—like feeding her femininity by making sure her hair and nails were always clean and done nicely. Not just clipped in a hurry, but done in a way that made her feel presentable. And Terri did in fact always look radiant and well put together, even if done simply. She never looked sick or unkempt. It said a lot about him that he understood this and did something about it. He knew what it took to make her feel like a lady, in spite of the indignity of being shut down one muscle at a time into a near lifeless existence. He absolutely understood.

That day, by the time he was ready to leave us, the tears had stopped and been replaced with his smile. It had taken a while, but he was back to being Robert, and left us with his signature "It'll all work out" mantra. "Man ... you're good," is all I could say.

Terri's freak accident came some months after. It was September 1, 2006. The evening before, we had all celebrated Alex's sixteenth birthday at a neighborhood Japanese restaurant, just ten minutes from our home. We chose one of the larger tables alongside the wall so as to give us more room for Terri's wheelchair. We enjoyed our sushi and sashimi, laughing and joking and enjoying our son's special occasion as if we hadn't a care in the world. Patty and her four kids had also joined us. Next to us was a window. We were still on daylight savings time, and I remember the low evening sun glowing warmly on Terri's face as she smiled at her firstborn being serenaded by the restaurant staff. In spite of the ALS, in spite of all that had come with it, I thought my family never looked happier.

The following day Patty came over to give Terri her usual massage and stretch session. After letting Patty in and helping her set up her table, I returned to the kitchen, where I was preparing Terri's green smoothie lunch. She would have it once her massage was over. Behind me on the television, the perky voice of the meteorologist was coming through softly in the background.

Then about ten minutes later, a scream pierced through the house like an arrow. It was Patty. I spun around from where I was standing at the counter and ran into the room. Before me was a horror scene. Bright red blood was splattered on the floor and walls. Patty was crying and gasping, hunched over her sister, who lay motionless on the floor. I flew to Terri and carefully turned her around. What I saw was enough to make me want to faint on the spot. Her face was smashed and bloodied. I called her name until I heard her groan. Meanwhile, Patty had already jumped on the phone to call 911.

Patty was still shaking as she told us later that it had all happened the second she turned her back to get a pillow for Terri's legs. "I left her lying there on her side," said Patty. "I swear all I did was turn and reach for the pillow behind me. But before I could spin back around, I heard that sick thud."

Unable to use her arms or legs to break the fall, Terri had plummeted to the floor straight onto her face. My stomach felt as if it had flown up to my throat and lodged itself there permanently. I wanted to scream but could barely speak. Wasn't it quite enough that she was dying from one of the most cruel of diseases? Why was this happening to her?

We rushed her by ambulance to the emergency room at Baptist Hospital. By the time we pulled in, her face had swollen so badly, she was almost unrecognizable. I swallowed my tears and remained calm. The last thing I wanted to do was send her into a panic. Since no one but I could communicate with her at this point, I remained glued to her the entire time. When X-rays showed that she had sustained multiple fractures to her face, the doctors scheduled her for surgery immediately.

As they wheeled her away, I sank into a seat in the lobby and stared at the ceiling. Once again life had switched on a dime … as if the happiness we had held in our hands yesterday was nothing more than an illusion.

Two hours later, she emerged from surgery. The titanium pins the doctors had inserted into her jaw forced them to put in a trachea tube for breathing while her mouth recovered, as well as a feeding tube in her stomach. Two weeks, said the surgeon, was the minimum length of time she'd need to stay in intensive care due to the ALS complication. Terri did in fact develop pneumonia after the surgery. At first the doctors wanted to perform a CT scan, but Terri refused, insisting that all she needed to do was to treat it holistically, which she did. I went home to retrieve the ingredients she needed, which included silver. Two days later, the pneumonia began to subside.

Once again I made arrangements so I could stay by her side. By now we had almost gotten to the point where I could tell what she needed just by reading her eyes. Where the nurses allowed it, I took over some of their duties, such as changing Terri and cleaning her after she relieved herself. At first she tried the hospital food, but as it was milk-based, she developed congestion that made her uncomfortable. I told them to cancel all meals, and I hopped into my car to go home to prepare her green smoothies with organic vegetables. Ironically, in the end Terri spent all of two nights in intensive care. The swelling that had taken over her face had calmed significantly. Her general health, much to the doctors' surprise, was otherwise textbook perfect—cholesterol, blood pressure; even her bowel movements returned immediately and were considered "quite satisfactory." The doctors were impressed at what turned out to be an easy postoperative phase. Other than the ALS, they said, Terri was the picture of health.

After a week of her recuperating in post-intensive care, we were told we could prepare to leave the hospital. Terri, however, was not happy. She wanted the feeding tube removed. I went to the doctors with her request. Not surprisingly, they insisted that it was best she keep it in. Under the circumstances, they argued, the tube should stay. She may well need it down the road. Terri and I understood only too well where they were coming from. She reluctantly agreed and left the hospital. But a week later she was still insisting that it be removed. She wanted to be able to taste food, she said. She wanted no tubes of any kind. They tried again to talk her out of it, but she remained steadfast. I was there merely to interpret for their patient. And their patient, as sick as she was, knew exactly what she wanted. She wasn't going to give up her wishes just because she had only a few years to live and had lost her ability to communicate. What most didn't understand was this: Terri was determined that she be treated like other patients who felt they had a right to ask for what they wanted. In the end the tube was removed.

That New Year's Eve, we went to a friend's party being held at the Palmetto Bay Village Center. Surrounded by a couple hundred friends and acquaintances, I took my wife out onto the dance floor in her wheelchair. Again I lifted her out of her chair and held her in my arms while allowing her feet to rest on mine. We danced with smiles on our faces. I kissed her on her cheek and told her she had always been my favorite dance partner. Always light on her feet, I said. It would be the last time we'd dance together.

It is during the worst times of your life that you will see the true colors of the people who say that they care for you.

—Ritu Ghatourey

Chapter 15

An Iota of Hope Is Still Hope

Ten miles.
Don't stop now.
Twelve miles.
No time to quit.
The pain is all in your mind.
Ignore it.
You can do it.
You have to.
You will.

As time went on and the disease progressed, we limited our social outings to only those that we felt were manageable. It had nothing to do with ego or Terri feeling sorry for herself. She had accepted her situation, plain and simple. This was her lot in life, and all she could do was work with it. And even though she was throwing everything she could at her ALS, she had made her peace with it.

As for me, even though it was clear that the disease was inexorably taking her, in my mind I still refused to see her as an invalid. She remained now what she had always been—my wife and life partner.

The simple fact was that she was deteriorating, which made it all the harder to keep her physically comfortable in public. Now, more than ever, we had to pay attention to the smallest detail. Terri did her best to help us, one slowly typed out word at a time:

When head bent over backward, I cry because hurts.
Must bend head to swallow saliva.
When I cough, hold me firmly by shoulders.
Leg hurts when turned out.
Need walk movement.
Use reformer under Pilates table. Easy to set up.
Right foot curves because outer thigh muscles weak."
When diet or thoughts are acid, body produces cholesterol
over joints and blood vessels to protect from acid.

With her inability to communicate with anyone but the boys and me, well-meaning friends were beginning to approach her as if the disease had also robbed her of intelligence. The greetings often came in an elevated tone, as if she had also lost her hearing.

Hel-lo, Ter-ri!! Do … you … re-mem-ber me?!

She would look at me with a twinkle in her eye and a huge smile on her face as if to say, "Here we go again!" Of course, the unsuspecting friend would think that Terri was just truly pleased to see them, which she always was. Let me be clear on this point. Terri exhibited supreme patience with those who came her way. She understood and appreciated that it wasn't every day you had a friend with a disease that locks you down and changes everything about you, save for your brain. So, no, she never ceased to be gracious about it. But after a while I'd preempt all visits with a quick and friendly reminder that she was neither deaf nor slow. "She may be trapped in her body, but she's still the same Terri,"

I'd tell them. "She remembers everything about you and every little secret you've ever shared with her. ALS has not claimed the part of her that makes her the person she is."

That was the one thing I always told her. "Terri, I'd rather have your brain intact and your body broken than the reverse. What is our body without our memories and our thoughts? Nothing but flesh."

I continued to devote my time to my wife. And when I say that, I mean that we were almost always in the same room together, interacting. I wasn't just sitting there whiling away the time and doing my own thing to keep myself occupied. Sometimes we'd watch television—the news, movies, anything that was entertaining or distracting. Terri was now more compassionate than ever, and I'd often see the tears in her eyes if she saw someone suffering. It wasn't that she hadn't been sensitive before, but now she didn't hold back. She just let the tears trickle down with the kind of sorrow normally reserved for someone close.

Other times, I'd deejay music for her on the laptop computer. I knew her favorites and played them either as a surprise or at her request. Love songs now meant more to us than they ever did. No longer was it just about the melody. I'd choose them carefully to tell her—in words that were beyond my capability—that I would not have changed a thing even if I had known before we married that ALS was going to be part of the plan.

As time went on, I'd hear comments about Robert being forced to live as a recluse—trapped in a prison, they said—and there was more open wondering about why I didn't now put my wife in a home. Clearly she had gotten so much worse, they weighed in. Everyone could see that. I dismissed them all. I understood that it looked crazy. I admit that on some levels it was. I was a twenty-four-hour private solo nurse with only the occasional relief staff or resting period. On call, day in, day out. But even then I knew that it would have broken all our hearts if I had sent her away. I may have found myself in a prison of sorts, but so was she—and it was my choice to sit next to her, even though my escape hatch was wide open.

"For better or for worse" was our promise. We had had more than our fair share of better. A surplus. And now worse was here. If I couldn't make the others see that love does what love is supposed to be—truly unconditional—then there was no use trying to explain. And as much as I wished that ALS had never knocked on our door, as much as I prayed, dreamed, and hoped that it would just vanish, I felt, in some strange way, that I had been destined to look after this woman. It was a job for which I'd have never considered myself qualified. But there were moments—especially whenever I saw her smile—when I felt almost blessed for having been chosen.

With Terri sleeping in shorter spurts now, my days and nights became more or less indecipherable. I continued to struggle with it, trying to sleep whenever she did. It wasn't all under control, and we didn't always get it right. Fatigue got the better of us every now and then. For instance, one night while lifting her out of bed to take her to the bathroom for the third time, I was so groggy that I lost my balance and caused us both to go crashing to the floor. Neither of us was hurt, but it was a clear indication that my energy tank was being depleted. Every now and then I'd find myself nodding off on the couch while sitting. I'd always snap out of it with a start, quickly glancing to see if Terri saw me, which she usually did. But then she'd give me an almost comforting look mixed with love, concern, and sadness. I'd always return it with a broad smile. I never wanted her to see me be anything but happy, even if she knew I had my moments.

One morning I got up as usual to get the boys ready for school. That particular day, Terri was still asleep when my alarm went off at the usual 5:00 a.m. Up until then I had made it a habit to wake her up, take her to the bathroom, and get her settled in her wheelchair in front of her computer before leaving the house. Even though the drive to and from the school was no more than twenty minutes, Terri preferred to be upright in her wheelchair when alone, rather than lying down and unable to move. At least then she could e-mail me if there was a problem—or, in her case, an emergency.

But that morning ... I suppose I was just too tired to make that extra effort. Worse, we were running late for some silly reason. One thing led to another. Before I knew it, I had made the split-second decision to take a shortcut and let her sleep. *It's only twenty minutes,* I told myself. *I'll come straight home. It'll be fine.* But when I returned home, I opened the front door to hear Terri screaming in sheer terror. I ran to the bedroom, where she lay on her bed crying like a panicked child who had lost her parent in a crowd. I scanned her quickly to see that she was unhurt, and I hugged her close.

"Terri! Oh, my God, honey, what's wrong?" I asked. "Are you hurt? Did something happen?"

But she was not hurt, just frightened. She had awakened to find herself completely alone in a very still house. And even though logic told her that I'd be back soon, even though she knew that it would be only a matter of minutes before she saw my face, even though she knew that I'd never be careless and leave her for longer than I had to, the terror in her escaped the only way it could. It was the most wounded sound I'd ever heard. After that day, I never left her alone again. Not even for a minute.

The disease continued to strengthen like a tidal wave churning into itself, growing before our very eyes. By now we had begun to use a special container that allowed her to urinate by just standing above her chair, similar to the one used in hospitals. It was not the most ideal arrangement, but it reduced significantly the time it took us to get Terri to the toilet. It also helped to conserve my energy, which had already slipped below the halfway mark. Bathing her and washing her hair was a nightly ritual that we never missed, no matter how tired I was, and no matter how late it was.

It was Terri's research on the Internet that led us to discover another useful aid called a pivot disk, or "transfer wheel." Looking a lot like a huge lazy Susan, this particular contraption became a lifesaver when it came to bathing her. Terri typed out the instructions for me, outlining how we'd use the transfer wheel. By now she stood as a rag doll would—bent forward at the waist if not held up by someone. Each night I'd remove her clothing, place her on the disc, spin her around slowly, and slide her into the chair in the shower. The chair had no headrest, so we came up with a makeshift one that did the job. After her bath was over, I'd repeat the motion, this time transferring her into another chair outside the shower that sat waiting for her, where I toweled her dry like a spa client. I continued to pamper her during her bath time as I always had, always touching her with a tenderness that was matched with a smile on my face and in my eyes. The attention I gave her still had its effect, and we continued to make love as if ALS were nothing more than an inconvenience. And when I say that, I mean that Terri wasn't just going through the motions to please me. No. She responded with the fire and honesty of a woman who wanted to feel pleasure.

If ALS taught me anything, it was that romance for a woman starts mostly in the mind. If you can attract her mind, if you can get her attention up there, then you have the power to please her—really please her—anywhere. Many men know how to capture a woman's heart, they say, but few know how to treasure and keep it. That's where most fail.

Later that year, some friends of ours mentioned a trip they had planned to visit an Indian tribe's healing ranch in Sedona, Arizona. I saw Terri's eyes light up in a way that I hadn't seen in a while. I saw fresh hope in them again. I'll admit now that in my heart of hearts I didn't hold out much hope for this ranch, as enthusiastic as our friends were. But I wasn't about to tell Terri that. I wasn't about to tell her to stop dreaming for a cure. No one wanted her well again more than I did. So I supported anything she wanted. If it gave her a whiff of hope, even at this stage—when it was clear she was inches away from being swallowed whole—I was there for her.

I remember marveling at how life had changed us in that fundamental way. Before ALS, I was the dreamer, and Terri was the practical one. Now we had switched roles. I booked the trip so she could dream.

Being deeply loved by someone gives you strength,
while loving someone deeply gives you courage.

—Lao Tzu

CHAPTER 16

Trapped in a Miracle

Terri's hands belonged to her until 2008, after which they were the property of her ALS.

They were now too heavy for her to use her laptop computer or to feed herself. She was also having difficulty lifting or holding her head up. The only good news we had was the seeming disappearance of her spasticity. I should mention that after having lost and regained her bowel movement urges and bladder control several years before, she never did lose them again. We took great encouragement from this and from the fact that she still had not had another respiratory emergency. Terri gave full credit to her change in diet and holistic approach. She remained unbending in her determination to stick with it for as long as it was helping her, in even the smallest way. She had no argument from me. I continued to prepare all her organic vegan meals and made sure that she got her massages and stretches on a regular basis between Patty and me.

But now communication with Terri was reduced to her whispering one letter at a time. It was a task that proved to be difficult for her and whoever was taking down her notes:

If can't figure out letter I want, say alphabet to me and watch my eyes.

She had almost nothing left with which to make her voice heard in a world that still continued to march forward at full throttle—a pace that had once been hers. At her request, I bought her an audio book that taught readers how to strengthen the mind, called *A Course in Miracles*. She followed the entire book and began practicing meditation several times a day while listening to Indian mantra music. A group by the name of Deva Premal had become her favorite. For someone who could not move much more than her eyelids, she'd never traveled as far in her mind as she did now.

"It's all up to us," she said to me one day, letter by painful letter, after having completed the course. "Book says our minds must join and make wish come true. We can do this. We either choose to be happy or not. I choose happiness. Cannot change ALS. Cannot change outcome. Can change my attitude. But could not have come this far without you, Robert. Would have given up already if not for you. Maybe going through worst experience of my life. Perhaps won't survive. But at least can say that while was alive, I was loved. Thank you."

From that moment on, she went within to find her peace. Inside I went to pieces for her, while on the outside, I became her everything: her legs, hands, and mind reader. I don't exaggerate when I say that we had developed a near telepathic energy between us. It had gotten to the point where I would just know, somehow, exactly what she needed and when. I could literally look at her and feel that her left forearm needed to be rubbed, or that the spot on her head just above her ear needed to be scratched. I can't explain how this came to be. All I can say is that somehow our frequencies had become so honed, so intertwined and connected, that it was as if we had become the other's twin.

Now if she needed something, *anything*, she had to rely on me to either know it instinctively, or to have me check constantly by asking her these and other questions. The answer was either blink once for "yes" or twice for "no":

Terri, do you need me to move the cushion behind your back?
Are you ready for your smoothie now?
Is your stomach feeling uncomfortable?

To be trapped, locked away, unable to communicate ... unable to do more than breathe and blink ... how did she not lose the one thing that was left? How did she not lose her sanity? For a person who had been reduced to what some would describe as a piece of furniture, Terri was teaching me more about mind power than I could have learned on my own. I consider myself a strong person. But I'll tell you this: had it been me in that chair, I don't think I could have continued to offer a smile to the world. Or to anyone, for that matter. But not Terri. She still celebrated the miracle of being alive every day.

Now there was no conversation with Terri. There were no small jokes. Not even simple sentences. No exchange of anything. Blood ran through her veins. Air came into and out of her lungs. She was alive. For the first time I began to miss her. I could see her, hold her, talk to her, but no longer could I hear her strong, reassuring voice or benefit from it even in written form. I ached to banter with her, to hear her opinion on something I was thinking of doing. I longed for the part of her she could not share. I longed for her mind. If it hurt me, it crippled our children. They could see their mother, touch her, talk to her, but they could no longer be soothed by her voice or rest easy from her reassuring advice. They couldn't have her. Not really.

Looking back, I would say that her inability to communicate was almost more devastating to us than the diagnosis itself. It was like seeing someone you love through a glass wall. You can look into her eyes, see the curve of her lips, but you can't hear her, can't really "be" with her. There were moments I thought that maybe now she would break or sink into some depression. But she never did. I never saw her cry or mope. I never sensed anger. She continued to eat whatever I brought her. And each and every morning, the first thing that remarkable woman did was greet me with a smile. This is how we lived for the next two years—in our own silent retreat.

It was now 2010. March would mark our twentieth wedding anniversary. As the weeks went by, I decided to broach the topic of having a small dinner party with friends to celebrate our special day. Okay, so she wouldn't be able to do more than sit there and observe. But wouldn't it still be great fun, I campaigned, if we filled our home with all the people we love? And I'd do all the work, I told her. She could just sit back and glare at me if I wasn't doing it right.

A single tear rolled down her face as she nodded with a smile so wide, it looked like she was laughing in stitches. I wasn't surprised that she agreed to it—the Terri I knew would never say no to such an event. But it still recharged my soul to know that this woman, who knew she was dying, still had enough hope and joy in her heart to allow room for an open celebration.

The promise of a happy gathering is a great distraction. We threw ourselves into planning our party of approximately fifty friends and family, and we inveigled the help of some of my immediate family members where the food was concerned. I kept my end of the bargain and did all the work, of course, but Terri surprised me by insisting on doing one thing. She wanted to write a speech to be delivered by me on her behalf. And so I sat with her while she dictated it to me one whispered letter at a time. The minute-long speech took us several hours to complete.

On the evening of our party, friends poured in and filled our home with more joy than we could have imagined. Terri beamed as one by one they squeezed and hugged her, many posing for pictures. She was the epitome of grace and let the love inside her shine through. While I don't doubt that many or most felt sorry for her, the sentiment did not stem from Terri herself. This is what she had to say to our gathering of loved ones:

A warm welcome to our wonderful family and friends. Twenty years ago, many of you celebrated our marriage with us. Twenty years and two awesome sons later, your presence is again required. They say opposites attract to teach each other lessons. I taught Robert to be somewhat organized and focused, and how to cook and clean. Robert taught me to be carefree, and the meaning of unconditional love. The true test of the mettle of friendship and family is the answer to the call in the hour of need. Life with Robert is feast or famine. In the darkest days of our lives, each one of you answered our call with such overwhelming generosity of pocket, time, and spirit, that God smiled. Robert and I thank you from the bottom of our hearts. As my soul mate and I make our spiritual journey in human bodies on this planet, we could not want a better soul tribe than you. Namaste.

P.S. From my vantage point seat, I can audit every return to the food table. I will make a full report to Robert's brother Richie, of anyone who comes by only once. Enjoy.

With our anniversary behind us, I continued to sit, stand, sleep, read, eat, and live by my wife's side. One day, while surfing through the television channels looking for something decent to entertain us, I happened upon the National Geographic Channel, a favorite of ours. I stopped, the remote still in my hand. On the television screen was a face I had seen several times before. He was an elderly gentleman, an intellect, and he was speaking through a computer-aided device. It was Stephen Hawking, the world-renowned English theoretical physicist. Diagnosed with ALS at twenty-one, he was still alive at seventy, and still in the business of sharing his brilliant mind with the world. That he had lived with ALS for so long gave me a surge of hope that I hadn't felt in years. But the immediate source of joy came from the fact that he was able to communicate. He did so though a special computer that allowed him to use his cheeks and eyes as his hands.

I immediately turned to look at Terri and ran to the computer to learn about the eye-gaze technology he was using. Within a matter of minutes, my research led me to a company by the name of DynaVox. And within a few minutes of researching the latter, I saw a name I knew well—Augie Nieto. Nieto was one of the owners of the company that manufactured the device I had seen Hawking using. I remember frowning at the unexpected surprise and sitting back in my chair to process it. But there was more. As I read on, I discovered that the reason for Nieto's involvement was personal. Incredibly, in March 2005, he, too, had been diagnosed with Lou Gehrig's disease.

I immediately felt the hair at the back of my neck prickle. How was this happening? Where did this full circle come from? And what did it all mean? Could it really be that a man—a stranger—with whom I had briefly crossed paths some twenty-plus years ago over a health-related interest, was now suffering from the very same disease as my wife? And could it really be that this man, this once-famous powerhouse and icon of health and strength, was the one person who could help her break free from the same prison of silence?

I didn't wait for my stomach to settle before getting in touch with Nieto's company. His eye-gaze device, the answer to Terri's prayers, was available at the tune of US $17,000. I held my head in my hands. We just didn't have that kind of money now, nor did we have medical insurance. I explained our situation to the person at the other end of the line. It was then that we were directed to the South Florida chapter of the ALS Association. They would be able to help. Further reading revealed that they had a "loan closet" that offered the use of all kinds of equipment for ALS patients, free of charge. There was a waiting list, it said, but the help was available.

I called the number shown and spoke with an angel by the name of Jessica Bianchi, the care coordinator of one of the association's support groups. Just hearing a cheerful voice and positive words at the other end of the line made my heart feel lighter. By August of that year, Jessica was at our doorstep with a DynaVox EyeMax computer. It may have just been an apparatus, it may have just been something that came out of a box, and it was certainly no cure. But for us it was like water for someone who had just crawled out of the desert after two years of cruel isolation.

I consider myself lucky that my eyes have been opened to the true nature of life. Mind you, I do not wish to spend one moment more in this chair if I can help it, but there is a certain detachment and wisdom coming from being trapped in your own body. Sometimes I hear people complaining over the silliest of things and I wish I could tell them do not worry or be afraid, for you are the master of your own physical reality. You can change your circumstances by changing your thoughts and how you see the world.

—Theresa Lee

CHAPTER 17

Of Sacrifice and Gratitude

Dear Robert, if January comes and I am not walking, I am asking you to divorce me and get on with your life. All I ask you to do is to pay for my care and put me somewhere pretty. It has been a long time, this ALS experience, and you deserve better. I thank you for taking such good care of me, even at the cost of your own health. But it is time for you to take care of your own needs now. I love you.

Theresa

Terri sent me this letter for the first time in December 2010. She would make the same request at approximately the same time each year for the next two years until her passing. I told her then what I would tell her each time she did this:

You just need more time, honey. Just hang in there. You're staying right here with me, with us, in your own home. You're not going anywhere and I will not divorce you.

This letter—this show of both hope and love despite the years of crippling illness—at first crushed me like an avalanche. To know that she *still* hoped, could still see herself walking despite the obvious progression and advanced stage of the disease; and to know that she loved me enough to want to give me a "normal" life even if it meant one of loneliness for her … the power of the two emotions both broke my heart and filled it with even more joy.

The truth was that I was bordering on a state of complete exhaustion. Did I feel sometimes that I could not physically go on? Yes. But while I had begun to seek outside help with the house, I had no intention of sending Terri to a nursing home. The bravery she showed in that letter only made me even more determined to make her feel loved until she took her very last breath.

I had always marveled at how magnificent trees look against the dark gray of an angry, stormy sky. It is then that the green of the leaves stands out the most. In many ways, this is what the backdrop of ALS did for Terri and me. It made the color of our love stand out stronger than ever.

To say that the DynaVox computer gave Terri back her life is to make too diluted a statement. She was, for all intents and purposes, a whole person again. Not only was she back in charge of her family, she started a blog and shared her voice with anyone who cared to hear about her experience. She expressed her happiness in a thank you letter to the ALS Association:

Dear Jessica,

I can't begin to tell you how this DynaVox EyeMax computer has changed my life, or thank you enough. My eyes have become stronger and I am a real pro at it now. We figured out how to use the e-mail and I got my life back. I can now talk with family and friends at home and across the world. I have gone from a living statue back to a wife, mother, sister, and friend. It has made life easier for me because now I can explain what I want and what I don't want. Now I can help Robert with the boys and the house. The buttons on the Internet were small and we couldn't figure out how to use it. So Robert e-mails the YouTube links or the websites and I am in heaven. I want to do a website or write an e-book, but have not found anybody to help me. The Microsoft Office on this computer is difficult to use, so I need someone to retype in Microsoft. But that is the least. Thank you, Jessica! Thank you so much! God bless you and the ALS Association a thousandfold. Robert can leave me for an hour or two now because now I can explain to anyone what I want them to do and how. Robert and I are closer and happier now because we can communicate. The family is so happy because I was the solutions person and now I can help everyone once again! Much love and blessings.

Theresa

The support we received from the local ALS Association went beyond our expectations, and it was a lifeline we treasured with relief and gratitude. Before ALS, I had considered myself a man of compassion. I had often donated time and money to those in need when I could. Looking back, I can see now that while I did these things because I knew it was the right thing to do, I can't say I fully grasped what it really meant to those on the receiving end. I don't think I ever stopped to think about how it felt—truly felt—to the one suffering.

But when ALS caused the tables to turn, I finally understood—really got—that when someone is hurting, in pain, and suffering, no matter the cause, there is no kinder act than validation. You do a world of good when you take time to acknowledge that person and his or her suffering. You make a powerful statement by opening your heart and offering a kind word, a hug, advice, or just an hour of companionship. Something. Anything. To know that you're not shipwrecked on a deserted island with whatever it is that's broken you can often mean the difference between complete despair and hope.

With the help we received from them, Terri was poised and ready to return the favor. She wrote this article for the ALS Association's newsletter:

Gratitude

I am so grateful for the ALS (Lou Gehrig's dis-ease) in my life over the past eleven years. It has taken me on an amazing journey that I would never have thought possible or envisioned.

When I received my diagnosis in 2002, it started me on a search into the realms of nutrition, herbal therapies, energetic healing, mind study, Eastern practices and philosophy, spirituality, and quantum physics. I did not always feel that way, but as the years went by and events unfolded in my life, I began to appreciate the life lessons ALS was teaching me, and also my family and friends. Before ALS, I was the typical superwoman managing several businesses while raising a family and juggling school, church, and social activities on a very hectic schedule. I was super-busy, super-stressed, and super-tired, hallmarks of a chronic overachiever. Then, thankfully, I got a wake-up call from ALS. I realize now that nothing else would have gotten my attention and made me slow down. Because of ALS, my focus is always now on a healthy lifestyle, and I keep health on the forefront of the family radar. This has kept them fairly healthy over the years.

Sometimes, I have counseled family and friends with serious or life-threatening illnesses on holistic treatments. Countless times, family and friends tell me, when life is coming at them fast, they would often think of me and find the courage to go on. It really makes me feel good to know that I can make a difference in people's lives. ALS gives only a small window of opportunity in which to allow a person to do his or her own research. In 2008, my arms became too heavy to use my laptop or write. I could whisper one letter at a time to my caregiver, but it was an arduous task for both of us. So I focused on doing guided meditations and an audio book by the name of *A Course in Miracles*. It is a course in mind training that teaches many new concepts, including the fact that our thoughts create our reality and our health. The course spoke of love and forgiveness in a new light that would change my life in the way I think and see the world.

Then the universe smiled on me. In August 2010, Jessica Bianchi from the ALS Association South Florida chapter visited me at my home in Miami. Jessica loaned me an eye gaze computer from the association's loan closet. Suddenly, I became a wife, a mom, a sister, a daughter, an aunt, and a friend once again. I had a voice, and a very loud one at that. I could interact with the family of humanity with dignity and without effort once again. I said the prayer at the family's Thanksgiving dinner. I could send e-mails, surf the Internet, and watch YouTube videos. I was in paradise. Thank you, God! I could continue to gather information for my cure. Thank you, Jessica; thank you, ALS Association. Now I could tell my wonderful caregiver husband, Robert, how to take even better care of me. I could also share what I was learning with Robert, family, and friends. I explained to them that all emotions stem from two basic emotions: love and fear. There are no private thoughts, and every thought creates the world around us. Robert is a quick learner, and I watched him transform our home, business partners, family, and friends by feeling and sending thoughts of love as he interacted with them.

As for me, my holistic lifestyle has extended my life span and improved the quality of my life. I don't require the usual accessories for ALS: no feeding tube, respirator, drugs, water thickener, or lifts. I enjoy excellent health, have not needed to see a doctor in years, and am drug-free. My spasticity has given way to extreme flexibility, breathing has improved, and coughs disappeared. I am an organic raw vegan, which has given me reverse aging and a glowing, flawless skin. Robert and I are closer and happier than ever in our twenty-one years of marriage along with our two sons, Alex and Justin.

They say gratitude is the most important emotion for healing apart from love. I know deep in my heart that ALS will soon depart from my body when it has accomplished all it came to teach me and have me do in this lifetime. And for that I am grateful.

—Theresa Lee

The woman of the house had returned. My wife, my friend, our boys' mother—we had her once again. I saw the effect on our children almost immediately. It was as if some of the fear had left their hearts now that their mom had returned. She was reachable. She picked up from where she had left off two years before, her voice stronger than it had ever been:

January 26, 2011, 8:39 p.m.

Robert, the photo of Justin hugging me is one of the rare ones with his eyes open. I think you should print one and put in his room. Maybe help cheer him up.

January 28, 2011, 9:36 a.m.

Good morning, honey. If Justin doesn't mind the almond milk, buy it. It is better for him. Cheeses are okay for his blood type but buy organic cheese such as farmers' feta, mozzarella, cheddar. Buy rice cakes instead of crackers. If you can find turkey burger instead of chicken, that would be good for the boys.

January 28, 2011, 6:09 p.m.

I am beginning to understand how the energy works. In quantum physics, they say our emotions/thoughts/DNA all affect the electrons in the atoms in our bodies and the environment around us. If we are happy and enjoy what we are doing, it causes the electrons to create more of what we are feeling. And it's the same if we are angry, sad, or bored. I will send you a link that explains it very well.

January 29, 2011, 11:19 a.m.

When you put me forward on the potty, I am slouching on my belly. Push both legs up to take weight off belly. Thanks. Love you.

January 29, 2011, 12:57 p.m.

Don't be afraid. Everything is in divine order.

February 6, 2011, 10:46 a.m.

When I hold down my head for a long time, it is hard to lift back up. My neck muscles get tired and can't lift head. I need to constantly lower head to swallow saliva. When I cough most times it is saliva gone down my air passage. You need to put cushion in shower chair to the extreme right. Last night I was sitting too far left and I could not brace my body to lift head. Please cut a thin piece of Tempur sponge and put at back of remote so it doesn't slide so easily. The vibration of the bed makes the pain go away in my bottom. I awake when the pain is too much. The pain comes from the blood unable to move because stay in one position too long.

February 17, 2011, 7:30 p.m.

Robert, I know you like to hear the words "I love you," but for me actions speak louder than words. When you take such great care in making sure to buy all my foods. When you take such great care in preparing my foods. When you take such great care in bathing me. When you take such great care in putting me to bed. When you take such great care to see that I am happy. When you become a recluse to take care of me. When I sit in weariness to give you time to nap. When I smile in spite of everything. When I refuse to complain in spite of the pain. When I make every effort to get better. When I refuse to give up on life. We say, "I love you" every hour, every day, every year. We don't need Valentine's Day or fancy cards to express our love. Our life together is the dance of love. We live love, and we breathe love. We are one soul united in love for all eternity.

—Theresa Lee

If there's one thing I've learned from the ALS, it's about letting go. When Terri got her voice back again through the DynaVox computer, as much as the surge of pure joy returned color to my cheeks, I knew in my heart that this was as good as it was going to get. It was not going to make her walk again, nor was it going to make the ALS disappear or subside. But that was fine. I accepted it and blessed it for what it was—one last chance to have as much of her as we could. And so I let go of all of it. I handed over to God and to the universe all the hopes for a cure, for a remission, for anything that would give my Terri her life back as it once was. I sent it all away and stood, now clothed only in faith, with my soul facing the winds of what was meant to be.

Death takes the body.
God takes the soul.
Our minds hold the memories.
Our heart keeps the love.
Our faith lets us know we will meet again.
—Nishan Panwar

CHAPTER 18

And Then We Let Go

In December 2012, I got the letter Terri had begun sending me two years earlier. Again I gave her the same answer. "You just need more time." But now my reply had a tone of emptiness about it that could not fool Terri. It fooled no one—including me. By now I had sailed past the line of exhaustion. I was hurting. I was breaking down physically with relentless headaches, eyes that burned from just sheer fatigue, legs that just could not hold me up. Sometimes I'd catch myself literally shaking. Part of me was now whispering that I should "let it be"—let her go if it was her time to leave this world and transition to the next. And, still, the other part of me wanted her to fight harder to stay with us a little while longer, even if it meant living in a body that no longer worked.

A few days after her last letter, she began experiencing chest pains. Minutes later after I dialed 911, the paramedics were at our doorstep. They confirmed that Terri was suffering from nothing more than gas pains, and that her vitals were actually good. When they explained that they were required to take her to the hospital, however, she smiled and politely refused, and thanked them for coming. I signed the disclaimer they presented.

Now petrified and convinced that I was not equipped to take care of her in the face of an emergency, I decided to get some additional help from a hospice team. I called VITAS. I didn't need them there every day just yet, I explained, as I certainly didn't think the end was coming soon, but I wanted to make sure they were ready to act should I need them. Once everything was arranged, they began visiting us every two weeks.

The source of my stress at this point was not just physical. I knew deep inside—in that cave where only you can hear your thoughts—that I had almost no more to give mentally. Now I doubted my decisions. Now I could no longer fake my way through with a mask of optimism and a smile. For the first time, I found myself with neither the energy nor the clarity of mind with which to take charge.

On January 16, Terri celebrated her fifty-sixth birthday. We had a small cake for her with a single candle. A few days later I went to her, my eyes filling with tears as I brushed the hair by her temples. "Terri," I said, "honey … I'm sorry. I don't think … I don't know if I can go on much longer. I need a break. I need to get some help with caring for you. I just can't go on alone now. I know you understand, but I just can't go on like this."

The guilt hit me like an instant fever the second I let the words escape. It wasn't that I thought she'd mind my having help. It was the possibility that she would read another message into it—that I no longer wanted her to fight for her life because I could no longer care for her as I once did. What does it do to someone when the person on whom they depend says that he or she has had enough? But I respected her enough to not lie. She deserved the truth. I was flat on the floor and barely had enough energy in me to raise my own head, let alone hold hers up. It was obvious to everyone. And it was especially clear to the person who knew me like no other that I had reached my limit. She saw that I was now falling asleep in front of her, waking up at 2:00 a.m. to bathe her because I had passed out cold on the couch. The dark patches under my eyes now looked like heavy rain clouds. As a backup to the hospice support, I made arrangements for some help from two other ladies. I would remedy this phase, I told myself. I just needed extra hands and eyes. I just needed a short break.

Up to this point, Terri was still able to use the computer to some degree, but now her neck had grown noticeably weaker. We all knew what this meant, but none of us said anything—not me, not the boys, not our family or friends—but I believe we all knew that the winds were about to shift. And when February arrived, they did. That's when Terri decided to end everything.

I know now in my heart that her decision came a week or two after I had told her I was tired. Suddenly it was taking me twice as long to feed her. At first I had assumed that it was the ALS progressing yet again and was now making the task of swallowing difficult for her. I insisted that we take her to the hospital to have the feeding tube reinserted, but she refused no matter how much I begged. After a while, I stopped trying to change her mind. I knew that I could have easily had it done. I could have just put her into the car and driven straight to the hospital. She could not have stopped me. But forcing Terri to do anything was not what we were about.

As I sat there, feeling desperate and panicked, I reminded myself that she had done everything in her power to prolong her time with us. It didn't occur to me then that she might have had this in mind the day she insisted the feeding tube be removed after her accident. It would not occur to me until months later that this was Terri exercising the last ounce of control she had left over her life—control over her death.

Her transition started on Monday, February 4. As the universe would have it, it coincided with the hospice's visit. The morning had begun with her usual green smoothie. But this time I noticed that she was now struggling to swallow even more than she had the week before. I dismissed the alarm that rose in me and started to coax her into drinking as if it was nothing. "Come on, honey," I said. "Just another few sips. You need to have more. You can do this." She drank less than half the glass.

Terri stared ahead as if not wanting to look at me. In her eyes I saw a distant, trancelike stare. It was neither sadness nor anger but a steely resolve. It frightened me enough that I didn't want to ask her what she was thinking. I didn't want confirmed what I knew to be the truth—that she had made up her mind to go. I knew this because she had not done that morning what she had done every day of her life since we met—smile.

I went about my chores in an uneasy silence. Later that day, I was adjusting the brace around her neck to make her more comfortable. Standing next to her, I was facing the wall with my back turned to the computer. Nadine, one of the ladies who had arrived just the day before, was also in the room, straightening out some laundry. I remember there being a distinct heaviness in the air—a sense of knowing. Nadine and I instinctively maintained our uneasy silence, speaking only when absolutely necessary. Then, minutes later, we heard the words through Terri's computer.

"Good-bye. Good-bye."

With my hands still on the neck brace, I held my breath as if wanting to remain undetected by some villain that had stolen into the room. If I stayed completely still, the words would float out through the window without finding me, I thought. After a few seconds, I resumed fixing the brace as if I hadn't heard anything at all. I wanted to neither protest nor consent. I just wanted it to pass. Nadine and I exchanged not a single word. Not even a look.

Then, slowly, I pulled back to face Terri. I lowered my body so we could make eye contact. Without saying a word, I looked into her eyes, summoning all the love I had ever felt for her since the day we met. We just looked at one another, speaking in a wordless exchange, telling each other that even though we were tired now, even though we were unable to beat this ALS, ALS didn't beat us. It never stood a chance against us. I kissed her on her forehead and pressed my face against hers, feeling the warmth of her skin, trying to commit to memory the feel and scent of her. I said a silent prayer as I held her, asking God to stand ready to receive my angel.

I asked the hospice nurses to stay. Then I called my sons. To this day I can't remember how I told them that they had only days left with their mother. Maybe hours. I can't hear the words in my head. But I can still feel the way they stuck in my throat, and the way my stomach rolled and pitched as I delivered the most heart-wrenching words my children would ever have to hear. Nothing prepares you for something like that. Nothing makes you feel smaller than giving your children hurtful news. We huddled together in silence, bracing each other for what we all knew was now just a matter of time. I got on the phone and began calling Terri's siblings and close friends. "Come now if you can," I told them. "It's time. She's ready."

And so our vigil began.

That day we took her out of her wheelchair for the very last time and moved her to her bed. Still hoping, we continued to try to give her water. But the more we tried, the more she refused to swallow. Even at her physical weakest, we were no match for her mental might. Out of desperation, we began pressing wet towels against her skin to help keep her hydrated. That evening we put her on a respirator and began administering morphine for the pain that would certainly come from starvation. Through a stream of tears, Alex and Justin took turns reading to her from the journal she had written for them. Their voices were weak from the sorrow that now gripped their hearts. They were barely able to mouth the words their mother had written before they had even spoken their first words. I watched as Terri allowed a single tear to escape.

On Tuesday I called a priest in to administer her last rites. I'm not sure if at the time I thought I was doing it for me, for Terri, or for us both. But it was what I felt was the right thing to do. Over the next three days, the doorbell would ring to announce the arrival of a close family member or friend who'd come to say his or her last good-bye. Her brother flew in from Toronto as soon as he got my call, and he tried his best to make her fight longer too. Would she, he begged, allow us to put her on a drip? She blinked "no."

Tears poured down the face of every visitor—and still Terri showed no emotion. I watched her just about the entire time as I continued to stay by her side, napping only an hour or two at most when I had to. As Terri drifted in and out of sleep, I did for her then what I had done for the twelve years before. I cared for her body. It was in the act of caring for my wife—ensuring that she could enjoy the dignity of being clean and comfortable—that I found a strange kind of happiness. It would hold me up in the last days of our life together.

Wednesday morning came. When I awakened from my nap, she was still sleeping. It was her second day without food and almost no water. Now she appeared thinner and weaker, her small frame showing more of the bones that lay beneath her withering skin. Her feet, once thick and swollen, now looked as if they could be snapped in two. The nurses explained that her organs were drawing water from different parts of her body. We immediately increased the morphine and began wetting her lips.

When Terri finally opened her eyes, I ran to her. At first she just looked at me. I said nothing and brushed her hair back softly. And then she gave me the gift I desperately wanted just one more time—her smile. My heart raced. I kissed her gently over and over again, whispering her name as if tasting my last drink of water. It would be her last smile. It was also her most beautiful.

I knew then that she had made her peace with leaving us. I did what instinct had me do—I smiled back at my beloved wife not just with my lips, but with my eyes and my heart. Without saying a word, we told each other that it was okay to let go now. We would all be okay. "I love you, Terri," I said to her for the last time. I would never again hear those words from her. I didn't need to. Her final act of ending her life so that I could begin mine again said more than a thousand "I love yous" ever could.

Much to everyone's amazement, Terri continued to hold on. Her eyes were now half-closed most of the time. We watched her breathe, her chest rising and falling like a slow, steady dance. For a moment on Thursday she had stopped breathing, and we all ran to her, crying, calling her name, and touching her. Moments later she started breathing again. We almost laughed a little. I told the boys that that was their mom—a brave warrior at heart. This was her last gift to us, I told them, one last reminder that we should always fight for what we want up to our last breath. And so, with only love to fuel her on, she stayed with us for two more precious days.

On Saturday, February 9, at exactly 10:29 p.m., Theresa Angella Lee became our guardian angel. I had the honor of holding her hand as she made her quiet transition from her earthly home to the one that awaited her. I kissed her face and whispered "good-bye." The boys, who had been crying the entire week, had no more tears to shed, and they took turns to kiss their mother for the very last time. She was still warm. I picked up a shawl she'd often used and rested it across her chest. "I know you don't like to be cold," I said to her. There was not a sound in the room as I lit a few candles. I thought she would have liked that.

The nurses obliged me by delaying the funeral home's arrival by a few hours. Just a little more time, I said. I needed just a little more time with my Terri. When they arrived later that night, we heeded their suggestion that we not watch her being placed in the body bag. The boys went to their rooms. I felt a need to be outside. I walked through the front door and felt the coolness of the night air wash against my skin. There was not a sound to be heard as I stood there. I looked up to the sky and held my gaze at the stars.

Minutes later the front door opened again. Terri was leaving now. I watched as they wheeled her to the awaiting vehicle, its motor humming patiently. My throat tightened the second they shut the doors behind her. I stood there, frozen, yet wanting desperately to run and bring her back.

As the van pulled away into the quiet night, I finally wailed all the tears that happiness and love had not permitted me to release in the twelve years of her long and brave good-bye.

We did it.
The marathon is over.
We can stop running.
Let's rest now.
Just rest.

And when life gives you more than you can handle or bear,
Just remember, my friend, the solution is more love and less fear.

—Theresa Lee

Epilogue

In the days, weeks, and months that followed my wife's passing, I'd almost always be asked the question "Robert, how are you coping?" It was usually presented with the assumption that I was still in mourning and languishing in sadness. And each time I'd give the reply that lived in my heart. "I'm happy," I'd almost always say to the inquirer with a full smile. "I'm at peace." Most times I'd be met by a look of complete surprise.

I suppose my reply is not the one most would expect to hear, given how much I loved and adored my wife. The truth is, I've missed Terri every day since she took her last breath. At the time of the writing of this epilogue, the one-year anniversary of her passing is fast approaching, and I still miss her with every fiber of my being. Within minutes of my awakening each morning, my mind reaches for her. Images of her and thoughts about what she'd say or do float around me as I go about my day, living my new life without the woman who put the wind in my sails. I still wish that ALS had not taken her away from her children and me. I miss and long for everything she was—mother to our children, my wife, my friend, and amazing human being. I miss the sound of her voice, the feel of her skin, her constant companionship, and the love she had for our family. She was an incredible source of energy for anyone who was lucky enough to call her "friend," or those who knew her even casually. There's nothing I wouldn't give or sacrifice to have her back.

But in my heart of hearts, I know and accept that the experience we went through together was meant to be. I understand that it happened for a higher purpose. I now go about my life feeding off this knowledge. It keeps me moving forward with a smile on my face and in my heart. It keeps me in that serene place where only love and compassion reside. We had a fantastic journey together, Terri and I—a difficult one, to be sure, but then I can only assume that somehow the universe knew we were up to the challenge. And I'd say we did fairly well. I'd say we were *wassi*.

And so I tell those who ask how I'm doing, that Terri's last selfless act of love fuels me on. She could have stayed. She could have agreed to let medical technology prolong her life, if even for just a bit longer. But she loved us enough to want our lives restored to what they had been before ALS. She wanted that for our children and for me, more than an extension of her own life. She filled me with unconditional love—enough to last me *my* lifetime. I have no intention of wasting a single moment. In fact, I plan on making her proud from where she now sits, watching me pay forward everything our experience has taught us.

On February 16, 2013, we held the first of two services to celebrate her life. The first was held in Miami, while the second took place in Ocho Rios, Jamaica. Between the two, many came to pay their last respects to the woman I had the privilege of calling my wife. On both occasions, as I stood there delivering my tribute to her, I was filled with an understanding that the bravery she had shown in the face of a most cruel adversary had been an inspiration to more persons than I could have ever imagined. Looking out at the sea of faces, I was filled with a sense of love and pride that I often return to in the rare moment I catch myself feeling even a hint of melancholy.

That Terri was able to feel and share happiness—real happiness—in spite of knowing that her life was to be cut short can be attributed to two reasons. The first was her incredible mind-set. Terri's mental strength will forever serve as an example to those who watched her live, love, and even laugh through ALS. Once she accepted her lot in life, she wasted little of her precious time wallowing in self-pity. I can think of many a reason for which to be proud of her. That, I would say, ranks among the biggest. The second reason for her happiness lay in simple love. I still maintain that had she not felt the love she did from her family, friends, children, and me, she would not have wanted to stay for as long as she did. And it is important to know that she *lived* in spite of the disease. She lived each day she was blessed with another chance to make the most of what she had.

This is the other message I want readers to take from this book and our story. Know this: money makes life comfortable and easier. No question about that. But the only richness that can give you true peace of mind is the kind you find in your heart. You can have all the latest gadgets that make you the envy of your peers, the fanciest cars that turn heads on the highway, the most elaborate houses found only in glossy magazines, jewels that shine brighter than the sun itself, and a lifestyle that rivals that of a Hollywood celebrity. You can have all this, tenfold. But if you don't have love in your life—real, unconditional love from someone who wants only the best for you, who wants you to grow on *your* terms, who wants all your hopes and dreams to come to fruition, who puts your happiness before his or her own—then you have nothing.

We all agree that life is short. It's too short, I say, for time to be wasted on sadness. We've all been put on this earth to fulfill our life purpose. So find a way to fill your days with purpose. It differs for each of us. Terri's was to show the incredible power of the mind. Mine—I maintain—is to show the power of unconditional love. I will tell you to this day, that I loved Terri in a way that only action could have shown. Had she decided at any point in our marriage that she'd have been happier without me, I'd have honored her wishes as a man who loved her, and not one who felt he owned her—because for me, her happiness came before mine. Her joy. Her peace of mind. That is my definition of unconditional love. And the side effect of giving unconditional love is this: what you give is what you'll receive.

I suppose I could choose to be angry at the world for what we went through. There's no denying that ALS forever changed our lives. If I have one regret, it is that our sons will have to live with the painful memory of their mother's slow and wretched deterioration. It's not something any child should have to live through, and I pray every day for my sons. I pray that their lives will be enriched by what they endured. I can only hope that they'll honor their mother's example—and turn a tragedy into a triumph. I hope that as they approach adulthood and begin their own life adventures, her early death will serve as a reminder that time is a terrible gift to waste. I also hope that they'll forgive me if my decision to be their mother's caregiver hurt them in any way. Life had thrown a cruel choice at my feet. I may have made some missteps, but I want them to know that my heart was where it should have been.

Their road to recovery still continues. I am staying as close to them as I can to see them through their journey to a life of renewed happiness. I wish for them a gentler path from here on. I wish for them a life of compassion. I pray that they will encounter kindness along the way—kindness and patience from friends, employers, coworkers, family, and, most important of all, strangers. I acknowledge that my sons suffered even more than I did. All I want for them now are steady winds and blue skies.

As you go about your daily lives, mingling with others, remind yourself that you can't possibly know what burden the people standing next to you may be carrying. Perhaps they've had a great day. Perhaps they've just received sad news, possibly the most devastating blow of their lives. Maybe they're struggling with depression or a condition beyond their control. If you have it in you to put your hand on their shoulder or to say a kind word, I encourage you to do so. It may only take a few seconds, but the effect lasts so much longer. It's a powerful gift to be able to lift someone else's spirits. You may, in fact, be saving someone's life. The way we make others feel about *themselves*—that is the true measure of a human being.

Today, I make it a point to ensure that every encounter I have with other people is a positive one. I look them in the eye. I say "hello" or "thank you" or "have a great day," and mean it. The gesture is not always appreciated by the recipient—some are either too busy or too disconnected to feel anything in what is usually just a fleeting interaction with a stranger. But I never consider it a waste of my time or energy. Good energy is the kind of virus you want to spread. When the student is ready, the teacher will appear, they say. If I can make a difference to even one person in a day, a week, a month, I'm happy.

And, finally, a word of gratitude to the very special people who helped to pave a smoother path for our journey ... You are the beloved friends and family members to whom I will forever feel indebted for helping us when we needed it most. Your love and kindness came in many forms—time, talent, and, yes, treasure. I want you to know that your compassion will not be forgotten. You are part of the reason Terri and I were able to soldier on as we did. I especially want to thank those who took the time to ask how *I* was doing through it all. You have no idea how it touched me that I was in your thoughts, even though I was not the one in a wheelchair and staring the end of my life in the face. You will never know how the strength of your words steadied me when I felt I was ready to fall. *Thank you.*

I had always lived life without much room for fear. Now, with Terri's love and example to guide me, I find that I am living in an even stronger state of fearlessness. I am taking those leaps of faith more than ever before, and I find that the universe is responding to my output. This has given me such incredible joy. It gives me reason to smile just about every day I awaken. And I know that wherever Terri is now, she's still smiling with me.

How ALS Lived with Me for Twelve Years

Health Tips and Observations
By Theresa Lee

Health Tips and Observations

This book would not be complete without hearing from Terri herself. As I've already incorporated some of her notes into the main body of the book, I'll save the reader from as much repetition as possible and set out below new information she had gathered during the course of her illness. These are not to be considered recommendations. I'll even preface it by acknowledging that some readers may find her beliefs controversial—but this is Terri in her own words, following her own mind and heart.

—Robert

Although it is a hell of a way to change your life, in some ways I'm grateful for ALS. I would not have learned all I now know and would still be busy chasing an illusion. I did not consciously choose the holistic path, because I was completely unaware of its existence. It was more a case of the holistic way of life finding me. I tried many products, healers, and therapies. With some I saw no noticeable effect, but that didn't mean they weren't any good. Maybe I didn't need them, or I was doing so many things at once that I couldn't attribute anything to a specific product or therapy. But I am sure they assisted my overall well-being. Those that had a major impact are described further in my notes. There are others I would have liked to try, but our financial situation was a limiting factor. ALS is a bottomless pit when it comes to money, and even if it doesn't strike the family's main income earner, the full-time care required usually takes a heavy toll over the years.

I had a totally open mind when I started on my research path. I soon learned to avoid most things endorsed by the FDA, the Heart Association, mainstream media, and studies and events funded by Wall Street corporations. Whenever anything was debunked or ridiculed, I took a closer look. I came to realize there is an organized effort to discredit anything that is effective, safe, with no side effects, cheap, and can replace a major marketed drug. I learned that most of the foods sold in supermarkets do not nourish the body and cause more harm than good, and that even water from the tap in some cases is cause for alarm. My innocence was about to be decimated!

While reading a recipe book on raw foods, I learned a little-known fact, which became my lifeline. It said the body renews itself every seven years. I thought to myself that maybe I could regenerate my motor neurons, even though the doctors said otherwise. I am an optimist; once upon a time, all the wise people thought the world was flat. I learned very early in life to never listen to the experts.

From the information I was gathering, there seemed to be three steps required to regain vibrant health. The first was to stop putting poisons and toxins in the body. The second was to remove the poisons and toxins already in my body. And the third was to nourish and regenerate the body. I never really had a conscious plan, but there seemed to be some kind of preordained divine plan I was following. In fact, every time I had a need, it was met—and many times in the most unexpected of ways. In 2000, when the first symptom of ALS appeared in my body, my sister Patrice called me to say that she had this sudden urge to study massage therapy, but her husband was upset at the idea. She nevertheless followed her inner guidance and started the course immediately. She and Robert became instrumental in my overall care.

The step that required poisons and toxins to be removed from the body came about unexpectedly. In 2003 I lost peristalsis movement in my colon, which meant that I had no urge to move my bowels. At the time I was doing a program that involved an Atkins-type diet. I had not yet learned of the raw diet or the effects of an acid diet. In addition to the heavy meat and cheese diet, I was making my breakfast smoothie with pasteurized orange juice. I believe with the already-poor condition of my colon, the extreme acidic diet overwhelmed my colon and caused it to stop working. Tests showed that there was no blockage in either my intestines or colon. Eventually hydrocolonic treatments remedied the problem. I had also learned that seawater is an excellent way to cleanse the body of toxins. I couldn't go into the sea, as I would get too cold and stiff, but I would sit in a chair on the sand and let the gentle waves splash around my legs and, at the same time, get a sunbath.

By that time I was on the raw diet, which was also detoxifying my body. I went through a year of detoxification therapies. Between the raw diet, hydrocolonic therapy, reflexology, footbath therapy, coffee enemas, cat's claw, and soaking in the sunshine and seawater, it worked! After nearly a year, I finally regained peristalsis movement in my colon. I was overjoyed! We don't appreciate our bodily functions until we lose them. Not only did it come back, but it came back more healthy and regular and has remained so. Most times I now say a prayer of gratitude whenever I have a movement.

Detoxifying the body is an ongoing process. It takes a long time to bring the body back to its natural, pristine state. Before my body had become too stiff and I could still sit in a bathtub, I would love soaking in hot water and Epsom salts. It was relaxing and pulled the tiny parasites from my colon. I later discovered that sea salt is an excellent way to detoxify. It can be rubbed on the skin or added to the bathwater. For an herbal detoxification, I often had many fresh herbs pounded together, with water added. This mixture was then rubbed on my skin and accompanied by prayers for healing.

Ginger is a powerful healing spice used all over the world. It has antioxidant, anti-inflammatory, blood-thinning, cholesterol-lowering, and cancer-fighting properties, just to name a few. So while in Jamaica, I took advantage of this. *Panchakarma* is a series of cleansing and detoxing *ayurvedic* therapies from India. Warm sesame oil with various herbs was poured on my forehead. I was given a full-body massage with the same oil for approximately two weeks. This released the poisons and toxins into my gastrointestinal tract and nourished my tissues. The massage also relaxed my body and mind.

The third and last step to regenerate the physical body required rejuvenation and nourishment. I have been a raw vegan for about eight years. Sometimes I tried other diets, but for the most part I've stuck to this one. I started on the raw diet after reading a recipe book by Frederic Patenaude. He said the body regenerates itself every seven years in stages, with some parts doing so every three years, like the stomach lining. I also learned that cooking destroys the enzymes of raw food, which are needed by the body to digest and absorb the food. So to digest cooked food, the body has to utilize its own enzymes, which depletes enzymes necessary for healing the body and other necessary functions. Worse yet, eating processed food stripped of its minerals and vitamins, such as white bread and rice, pulls on the body's own supply of vitamins and minerals to digest these poor-quality foods, and thus contributes to malnutrition. So as to give my body the best opportunity to heal, it seemed that a raw food diet was the logical choice.

However, in 2011, my body began to reject the raw food, and I discovered that everything needs to be taken in moderation. For about two years, I had very little physical therapy or exercise due to financial constraints. Nine years of ALS had taken a heavy toll on the family's finances. The lack of movement was affecting my lymph system and my spleen. Worse, according to Chinese beliefs, raw food weakens the spleen. So I started to incorporate grain and vegetable soups into my diet, which eventually corrected the problem with my spleen.

Along with the raw diet, I have incorporated aspects of other dietary practices as well. The natural hygiene diet says it is best to eat fresh fruits in the morning. At nights, the body repairs itself, which generates waste. This waste is eliminated from the body in the time frame of 6:00 a.m. to noon. Eating other foods stops the elimination process to digest these foods, as the body can do only one process at a time. Fresh fruits need no digestion by the stomach and are assimilated in the small intestines. So to give my body the maximum opportunity to remove waste, I eat only fresh fruit in the morning and a vegetable smoothie, until about 11:00 a.m.

The blood type diet is as the name implies. I was on and off this diet from about 2001. I have blood type B, which is the most difficult for this diet. I need to avoid most of the common foods consumed in a normal diet. Chicken and avocados cause my blood type to clump together, which then leads to other problems. Other foods to be avoided by the B blood type include soy, corn, canola oil, sesame seeds, tomatoes, peanuts, cashews, and more.

Over the years, I always had a severe pain in my right groin. Sometimes it went away or lessened. I never really understood the concept or the term "agglutination of the blood," a term used by the author and creator of the blood type diet. Then, in 2011, when my groin started to hurt, I had an epiphany. I realized that it was when my consumption of avocados and certain other foods on the B type "avoid" list was high that my groin would hurt.

I swore off all B-type avoid foods, and all my groin pains disappeared. The tendons in the groin area, which a physical therapist had described as "steel cables," completely relaxed and became pliable once again. My theory was that the "avoid foods" clumped the blood, which clogged or overwhelmed the lymph nodes in the groin, which then caused the pain.

There is some dispute regarding food combination. Some say it matters what food is eaten with what for proper digestion. For instance, one belief is that the stomach cannot efficiently digest starch with proteins. I don't know who is right, but I prefer to err on the side of prevention. Being a raw vegan takes me out of much of the controversy. The only rules I follow concern fruit. The food combination protocol says that fruit is to be eaten alone, and not after a meal. When fruit sits in the stomach waiting for the meal to be digested, it ferments and produces toxins such as formaldehyde. So I eat fruit alone or in a green smoothie with green leafy vegetables, which is the only food allowed with every food type.

Another aspect of diet to be taken into account is the alkalinity of the food. When the diet is too acid, it makes the body acid. The body has to be maintained at a pH level of 7.35 (alkaline) for perfect health. An acid body is the cause of all illnesses. The meat-heavy Western diet is very acid, as are some vegetarian diets with overconsumption of cheese and nuts. So the balance between alkaline and acidic foods is crucial to maintaining good health.

The last aspect of my composite dietary regimen comes from India. According to the ancient ayurvedic traditions, there are three types of body-mind constitutions based on the elements of nature: fire, water, air, and space. The body-mind types—or *doshas* as they are called—are *vata*, *pitta*, and *kapha*. *Vata* is space and air, *pitta* is fire and water, and *kapha* is earth and water. We all have one major and one minor *dosha*.

It is essential for good health to keep our *doshas* in balance through diet and lifestyle. To keep my *pitta-vatta dosha* in balance, I needed a salty, sour, sweet, heavy, and oily component to my diet. Over the years, I have gone through various stages of extremes of pepper or ginger or salt or bitter, or whatever my *doshas* craved at the time. Following *dosha* balancing has made my meals more satisfying and enjoyable. I find I need less food to satisfy my hunger, and I don't get as hungry between meals. I am calmer and more patient, and enjoy a better frame of mind. As the saying goes, you are what you eat!

It is not enough to rely on the diet to provide adequate nutrients for the body, especially for regeneration. With the advent of the discovery of fertilizers manufactured from crude oil, it was all downhill for mankind! Before chemical fertilizers, each food crop would contain over thirty nutrients; sadly, now they contain maybe three or four. So it is essential to supplement the modern diet with super-foods, healing herbs, and easy-to-absorb vitamins and minerals for optimum health.

Holistic remedies: Sometime in 2003, a friend recommended a healing program to me. This was my first encounter with the holistic world. A hair analysis was used to determine the nutritional status of the body. It was a very high-profile setup with radio programs and a well-appointed office location. My hair analysis revealed I was suffering from malnutrition with a high level of aluminum. I was very surprised, thinking I ate a normal balanced diet. I soon learned that quality was more essential than quantity in terms of the diet.

I was given a multitude of vitamin and mineral supplements in pill form. I was given somewhat of an Atkins-type diet to follow. At first my legs became warmer and softer to the touch, and then the improvements leveled off. Compared with the results of other food supplements I took later on in my journey to health, I was not impressed with these pill supplements, even though they were of premium brands. Then the acidic Atkins diet created havoc with my not-so-healthy gastrointestinal tract, and the peristalsis movement in my colon ceased.

I have tried so many supplements, herbs, and teas over the years, that I have forgotten many of them. But there were some that played an important part in my recovery. Most of these I discovered on, and bought from, the Internet. These were the early years of holistic nutrition on the Internet, so the websites were filled with information to educate the public. Those websites where the passion focused more on well-being and less on making money, offered cutting-edge and quality products. A few of these noteworthy websites include:

Sunfood.com (previously Rawfood.com)
WolfeClinic.com
MountainRose.com
MiracleSoap.com
SCDProbiotics.com
MEMinerals.com (Mother Earth Minerals)
Kehe.com
PlanetTachyon.com

They say the best things in life are free, and I am discovering that this is really true. A friend who is a master feng shui practitioner recently e-mailed me about a case study she came across while studying principles of Chinese medicine. They said that several hundred years ago, a girl became paralyzed and stiff. She could not walk or talk.

They dug a hole in her room and practically buried her. They gave her acupuncture and treated her spleen with herbs. According to Chinese medicine, the spleen governs the muscles. The girl was cured and was able to talk and walk once again.

Of course, I looked up "healing energy from the earth through the feet" on the Internet. Bingo! On TheNewAgeBlog.com, they explain the process of healing by burial in the earth. It can also be done at the beach, but there must be no one around except a friend to assist you. Dig a trench to accommodate your body and lie in it. Sawdust or leaves can be used to line the trench for softness. Wrap yourself in a cloth or sheet for protection from insects. The optimum time to stay buried is dawn to dusk, but if this is not possible, try to stay there for at least six hours. You should also fast the day before.

Other sites suggested that you can also obtain healing from the earth by touching a tree. You must ask the tree to share the energy it gets from the sun and the earth with you, and you must thank the tree after. If no trees are available, a metal pipe sunk into the ground will work too. If you are unable to go outside, the intent can work. Visualize roots going from your feet to the core of the earth, and the earth energy coming up the roots into your body.

As I was homebound and unable to move, my friend suggested I go in the backyard in my wheelchair and put my bare feet on the grass. I followed her suggestion, and by the third day, I noticed I had more energy; the fingers on the right hand, which had been sticking together, were now separating. I was also experiencing less pain and could speak louder and more clearly.

I go barefoot in the late evenings when the sun is not too hot, and stay out for about half an hour. My sweet caregiver husband, Robert, as always accommodates my every need. He does this even though he has to struggle with my power-chair on the uneven terrain of the backyard. To supplement my "barefooting," I add visualizations. I visualize energy from the cosmos entering at the back of my head and into my heart. Then I imagine it coming from the earth through the roots extending from my feet to the core of the earth. The earth energy floods my body and meets the energy from the cosmos in my heart. The two energies unite and come out through my chest and surround me.

Cushions: the best cushions are a brand called Allman, sold on the Internet. I have found them more comfortable than even the expensive air cushions. The big difference between ALS and spinal injuries is that with ALS, you still retain sensory feelings. Sitting for hours in one position over the years make your buttocks become quite tender and painful. Sometimes it feels like I am sitting on knife blades or in acid.

Hemp seeds: I started eating hemp seeds sometime in 2006. Of course, like most things, I learned about it on the Internet. Between 2008 and 2009, my muscles began feeling less spastic. I became so flexible, I was like a pretzel. I never knew the cause until I read an article that said that marijuana reduced spasticity in people with multiple sclerosis. Hemp seed is marijuana seed. It appears as if you can get the same benefits by eating hemp seeds, but the effects are permanent and not temporary, as is the case when you smoke it. I had found an alternative to the Rilutek drug prescribed for ALS, but without the harmful side effects and the big price tag. Apart from reducing spasticity, hemp seed is a super-food full of protein and omega-3 essential fatty acid. I consume hemp seed raw in my smoothies.

Pivot disk: This simple turning wheel made a big difference in my life. It allowed one person to care for me. It also enabled me to go without wearing disposable underwear, and to travel and go places. The pivot disk replaced the need for an expensive lift, which, from what I understand, can be dangerous to use and takes up a lot of space. I discovered it on the Internet in 2005. Seven years later, many in the conventional medical profession are still unaware of its existence.

Silver, zinc, and copper: I was introduced to silver as a natural antibiotic without all the side effects by an osteopath doctor in 2002. He tested me on a frequency machine that revealed the presence of a powerful microbe in my digestive tract. He used silver to remove it. Silver, zinc, and copper are powerful antibacterial agents. Silver kills not only bacteria, but over 650 viruses. Since I discovered silver, my family and I haven't had the flu. At most we've experienced mild symptoms for only one to three days. In 2006, I was in the hospital after fracturing my facial bones from a fall. The doctors used the opportunity to insert a feeding tube. This caused me to develop pneumonia. They wanted to do a CT scan or some such test. I refused and sent for my silver and zinc. By the next day, the pneumonia was gone.

I buy my minerals from Mother Earth Minerals. They are angstrom-size and taken under the tongue, where they are absorbed directly into the bloodstream. This is important, especially if you have absorption problems in the stomach. It is imperative that persons with ALS don't get the flu, as they are unable to cough up the mucus from the chest. So silver is vital for the prevention of the flu, especially in the early stages. Zinc doesn't kill viruses, but it prevents them from multiplying.

Live each moment in wonder and good cheer.

The past is gone and the future not yet here.

Laugh at life and keep God near.

Positive thoughts will bring endless health and wealth each year.

And when life gives you more than you can handle or bear,

Just remember, my friend, the solution is

more love, less fear.

—Theresa Lee